GLUTEN-FREE
ARTISAN
BREAD
IN A SNAP!

3 BONUSES INCLUDED

Emma Brooks

EMBRACING ZERO WASTE 🌱

In our effort to make this cookbook as environmentally friendly as possible, we've chosen to exclude images. By reducing the resources needed for printing and shipping, we aim to minimize our carbon footprint and help you embrace a zero-waste lifestyle.

This decision aligns with our values of sustainability and responsible living. We hope that, through these recipes, you'll find inspiration to create beautiful, delicious meals while caring for our planet. Thank you for joining us on this journey towards a greener, more sustainable future.

SCAN THE QR CODE TO JOIN THE BAKING SISTERHOOD FACEBOOK GROUP!

CONTENT'S OVERVIEW

STEP INTO THE WORLD OF GLUTEN-FREE ARTISAN BREAD

Welcome to the inviting world of gluten-free artisan bread, where every loaf is a gateway to rediscovering the textures and flavors you've missed. I'm Emma, a passionate baker who has navigated the transition to gluten-free living, balancing the demands of work and home life while striving to serve delicious, nutritious meals that everyone can enjoy. If you've ever struggled to find gluten-free bread that truly satisfies or felt overwhelmed by the complexities of gluten-free baking, this book is your new kitchen companion.

In this journey, you'll find that crafting your own bread at home can be both straightforward and deeply rewarding. We'll delve into a collection of recipes designed for busy lives, ensuring you can enjoy homemade bread without dedicating your entire day to the kitchen. Think of this book as your personal guide, offering tips and techniques to master gluten-free bread with ease, all while making sure your culinary creations delight the taste buds and nourish the body.

Understanding the challenges of gluten-free diets, especially with the pervasive presence of processed alternatives, here you'll find recipes rich in wholesome, all-natural ingredients. These recipes not only promise great taste and perfect texture but are also kinder to your health and the environment. Let's embark on this delicious adventure together, turning simple ingredients into extraordinary breads that bring back the joy of eating well.

As we explore these recipes, remember that baking is as much about the process as it is about the delicious outcomes. Each recipe is an opportunity to learn, to experiment, and to share something wonderful with loved ones. So, let's begin crafting exceptional gluten-free breads that are as satisfying to make as they are to share. Welcome to a world where every grain, every blend, and every loaf is an expression of love and care. Welcome to the joyous, tasty realm of gluten-free artisan bread!

Emma Brooks

UNLOCK YOUR FREE FLOUR BLENDING STARTER GUIDE & 2 MORE BONUSES

Welcome to your journey into the world of gluten-free bread baking! As you dive into the pages of this cookbook, you'll discover how versatile and rewarding it is to bake with gluten-free ingredients. However, to truly master the art of gluten-free bread baking, you need a solid foundation, and that begins with understanding flour blending.

I am thrilled to offer you the most comprehensive guide to creating delicious gluten-free flour blends—absolutely free. This guide is packed with step-by-step instructions, tips, and troubleshooting advice to help you craft the perfect gluten-free flour blends.

To access this invaluable resource, simply scan the QR code below and embark on your path to becoming a gluten-free bread baking expert.

By the way, scanning the QR code will also grant you access to two additional bonus guides:

1. Texture Triumph Toolkit: Achieve the Texture of Real Bread Every Tim
2. Busy Baker's Bible: 10 Time-Saving Hacks for Effortless Gluten-Free Baking

GLUTEN-FREE BREAD BAKING?

Gluten is a protein found primarily in wheat, barley, and rye. It acts as a binding agent within flour, helping dough to rise by trapping gas bubbles during fermentation. Gluten imparts bread with its characteristic chewy texture and elasticity. When kneaded, gluten strands stretch and strengthen, contributing to the structure and shape of the bread.

For many, the choice to go gluten-free stems from necessity due to celiac disease or gluten sensitivity, which can cause adverse health effects when gluten is consumed. However, adopting a gluten-free lifestyle has a broader appeal, as many people report feeling healthier, experiencing less bloating, and having more energy, even if they don't have gluten sensitivity.

Gluten-free baking isn't just a means to avoid discomfort; it's an exploration into a variety of grain options that can enhance flavor and nutritional content. Ingredients like rice flour, tapioca starch, almond flour, and buckwheat not only enable those with gluten intolerance to enjoy baked goods but also introduce an array of textures and flavors to expand the palate.

Achieving the Texture and Flavor of "Real" Bread

Embracing gluten-free baking opens a world of culinary creativity. It invites you to experiment with diverse flours and discover new tastes and textures. Gluten-free bread can be just as satisfying, if not more so, than traditional bread. Each loaf you bake is not just nourishing for the body but also a triumph of baking science and art.

The key to successful gluten-free bread lies in the blend of flours used. No single gluten-free flour can replicate the properties of wheat flour alone, so blends are essential. A mix of heavier flours like almond or chickpea with lighter starches like potato or tapioca starch can mimic the heft and texture of wheat flour.

Since gluten-free dough lacks the natural elasticity of gluten, binders such as xanthan gum, guar gum, or psyllium husk are used to help give the dough structure and elasticity. These ingredients act as the "glue" that holds the bread together, ensuring it doesn't crumble when baked.

Advanced techniques such as longer fermentation times, proper hydration, and precise temperature control arc crucial in gluten-free baking. These methods help develop the flavors typically achieved through gluten development in traditional baking. We will explore these techniques in detail throughout this book.

STORING GLUTEN-FREE BAKED GOODS

Successfully baking gluten-free bread and pastries is just the first step in enjoying your homemade treats. Given the absence of preservatives and the nature of gluten-free ingredients, these baked goods often have a shorter shelf life than their gluten-containing counterparts.

Gluten-free baked items tend to dry out and stale faster due to their different starch and protein structures. Without gluten, the bread and pastries can't retain moisture as effectively, leading to quicker spoilage. Understanding this will help you better prepare for proper storage methods that can extend the enjoyment of your baked creations.

Cooling Before Storing
Always allow your gluten-free bread and pastries to cool completely before storing. Packing them away while they are still warm can lead to condensation within the storage container, making them soggy and promoting mold growth. Place them on a cooling rack that allows air to circulate freely around each piece.

Airtight Containers
For short-term storage, keep your gluten-free baked goods in airtight containers. These can be resealable plastic bags or containers with tight-fitting lids. By limiting exposure to air, you minimize the risk of drying out your bread or pastries. If using plastic bags, squeeze out as much air as possible before sealing.

Refrigeration
While refrigeration can help prevent mold, it can also cause gluten-free bread to become dry and hard. If you must refrigerate, wrap your baked goods in a paper towel to absorb excess moisture and place them in an airtight container. This method can help maintain the quality for a few days.

Freezing for Longevity
Freezing is the best option for extending the shelf life of your gluten-free baked goods without sacrificing quality. Wrap each loaf or individual slices in plastic wrap, then place them in a heavy-duty freezer bag. Be sure to label each package with the date. Gluten-free bread can be frozen for up to 3 months. When ready to eat, thaw it at room temperature or gently warm it in an oven to revive its freshness and texture.

Reviving Gluten-Free Baked Goods
Revitalizing gluten-free bread and pastries can make them nearly as good as fresh. For bread, lightly sprinkle the loaf or slices with water and reheat in a preheated oven at 350°F

for about 5-10 minutes or until warm and slightly crisp. This method can help restore the crust's crispiness and the bread's soft interior.

For pastries, reheating them in an oven or toaster can bring back their delightful texture. Avoid using a microwave as it can make them tough and chewy.

Practical Tips
- Bread Bins: Use a bread bin for daily use bread. These bins help maintain an ideal humidity level, which is especially helpful in dry environments.
- Slice Before Freezing: For convenience, slice your bread before freezing. This way, you can take out just the amount you need without having to thaw the entire loaf.
- Keep Desiccants: When storing in containers, you can keep a small pack of desiccants to absorb any excess moisture that may lead to sogginess.

WHOLE GRAIN BREADS

AMARANTH BREAD

Preparation Time: 20 minutes
Cooking Time: 1 hour (60 minutes)

INGREDIENTS:
- 2 cups amaranth flour
- 1/2 cup brown rice flour
- 3 teaspoons gluten-free baking powder
- 1/2 teaspoon sea salt
- 4 large eggs
- 1/4 cup olive oil
- 2 tablespoons honey
- 1/4 cup lukewarm water
- Optional: seeds or nuts for topping

INSTRUCTIONS:
1. Preheat your oven to 350°F (180°C). Prepare a loaf pan by lightly greasing it with some olive oil or lining it with parchment paper for easy removal.
2. In a large mixing bowl, combine the amaranth flour, brown rice flour, baking powder, and sea salt. Whisk together until the ingredients are evenly distributed.
3. In a separate bowl, beat the eggs until they become frothy. Add the olive oil and honey into the beaten eggs and mix until well combined
4. Gradually add the wet ingredients into the dry ingredients. Mix until there are no dry spots. The dough might be slightly thicker than conventional bread doughs.
5. Gradually add the lukewarm water, mixing consistently. You may not need the entire amount of water, just enough to create a dough with a firm, but not too stiff, consistency.
6. Once the dough is well mixed, pour it into your prepared loaf pan. Gently shake the pan to ensure the dough sits evenly.
7. If desired, top the dough with your selected seeds or nuts.
8. Bake the bread in your preheated oven for approximately 1 hour, or until the top is golden brown and a skewer inserted into the center comes out clean.
9. Once baked, remove the bread from the oven and allow it to cool in the pan for about 10 minutes before transferring it to a wire rack to cool completely.
10. Slice and serve your gluten-free amaranth bread once it has cooled.

BROWN RICE BREAD

Preparation Time: 30 minutes

Cooking Time: 60 minutes

INGREDIENTS:
- 3 cups of brown rice flour
- 1 1/2 cups of potato starch
- 1/2 cup of tapioca flour
- 3 1/2 teaspoons of xanthan gum
- 1 tablespoon of salt
- 2 tablespoons of organic cane sugar
- 1/2 cup of dry milk powder
- 1 1/4 cups of lukewarm water
- 1/4 cup of extra-virgin olive oil
- 2 large eggs
- 1 teaspoon of cider vinegar
- 2 1/4 teaspoons of active dry yeast

INSTRUCTIONS:
1. In a large bowl, combine brown rice flour, potato starch, tapioca flour, xanthan gum, salt, sugar, and milk powder. Set aside.
2. In a separate, smaller bowl, combine lukewarm water and yeast. Stir until yeast is dissolved.
3. To the dry mixture, add in the olive oil, the eggs, and the apple cider vinegar. Mix well.
4. Gradually add in the yeast and water mixture to the large bowl. Mix well until a dough forms.
5. Grease a bread pan lightly with olive oil.
6. Pour the dough into the pan and smooth the top with a spatula.
7. Cover the pan with a clean kitchen towel and let the dough rise in a warm place for about 30 minutes or until it has doubled in size.
8. Preheat your oven to 400°F.
9. After the dough has risen, remove the towel and place the pan in the preheated oven.
10. Bake for 30 minutes or until the top of the bread is golden brown and a knife inserted into the center of the loaf comes out clean.
11. Wait about 10-15 minutes for the bread to cool before slicing into it.

BUCKWHEAT BREAD

Preparation Time: 15 minutes
Cooking Time: 45 minutes

INGREDIENTS:
- 2 1/4 cups buckwheat flour
- 1/4 cup arrowroot starch
- 1 package (1/4 ounce) instant yeast
- 2 teaspoons xanthan gum
- 1/2 teaspoon salt
- 1/4 cup honey
- 2 tablespoons olive oil
- 4 large eggs, room temperature
- 1 1/2 cups warm water (110°F to 115°F)

INSTRUCTIONS:
1. In a large mixing bowl, combine the buckwheat flour, arrowroot starch, instant yeast, xanthan gum, and salt.
2. In another bowl, mix the honey, olive oil and eggs together. Pour this mixture into the dry ingredients.
3. Gradually add warm water to this mix, while stirring continuously until a sticky dough forms.
4. Scoop the dough into a greased 9x5-inch loaf pan. Cover it with a towel and let it rise in a warm place until the dough reaches the top of the pan. This should take about 30 to 45 minutes.
5. Preheat your oven to 375°F.
6. Place the loaf pan in the preheated oven and bake for about 45 to 50 minutes or until the top is golden brown and a skewer inserted in the center of the bread comes out clean.
7. Remove the bread from the oven and let it cool on a wire rack for 10 minutes. After 10 minutes, remove the bread from the pan and let it cool completely on the wire rack.
8. Slice the gluten-free buckwheat bread and serve. You can enjoy it as is, make a sandwich, or toast it. This bread goes well with a variety of spreads like butter, jam, or cream cheese.
9. Remember, always store this bread in an airtight container or bread box when not used. Enjoy!

MILLET BREAD

Preparation Time: 15 minutes
Cooking Time: 40 minutes

INGREDIENTS:
- 2 cups of millet flour
- 1 cup of tapioca starch
- 1 tablespoon of xanthan gum
- 1 teaspoon of sea salt
- 1 tablespoon of baking powder
- 3 large eggs
- 1/4 cup of olive oil
- 1/4 cup of honey
- 1 cup of warm water
- 2 1/4 teaspoons of active dry yeast

INSTRUCTIONS:
1. Preheat your oven to 375°F (190°C) and lightly oil a 9x5 inch loaf pan.
2. In a large mixing bowl, combine the millet flour, tapioca starch, xanthan gum, sea salt, and baking powder. Stir until well mixed.
3. In a separate, smaller bowl, combine the eggs, olive oil, honey, warm water, and active dry yeast. Let sit for 5-10 minutes to allow the yeast to activate and foam up.
4. Once the yeast is activated, pour the wet mixture into the dry mixture, and stir until combined.
5. Pour the bread batter into your prepared loaf pan and smooth the top with a spatula.
6. Allow the dough to proof in a warm area for about 15 minutes. The dough should rise to the top of the pan.
7. Place the pan in the preheated oven and bake for about 40 minutes, or until the bread is golden and a toothpick inserted in the center comes out clean.
8. Allow the bread to cool in the pan for about 10 minutes, and then transfer to a wire rack to cool completely before slicing.

MULTIGRAIN BREAD

Preparation Time: 15 minutes
Cooking Time: 40 minutes

INGREDIENTS:
- 1 cup of warm water (about 110 degrees)
- 2 tablespoons of honey
- 2 1/4 teaspoons of active dry yeast
- 2 cups of gluten-free all-purpose flour
- 1 cup of gluten-free multigrain flour blend
- 1 teaspoon of xanthan gum (omit if your all-purpose flour blend includes it)

- 1 teaspoon of salt
- 1/4 cup of olive oil
- 2 large eggs
- 1 teaspoon of apple cider vinegar

INSTRUCTIONS:
1. First, in a small bowl, combine the warm water and honey. Stir until the honey is fully dissolved.
2. Sprinkle the yeast over the water, stir it lightly and let it sit for about 5 minutes until it is foamy.
3. In a large bowl, whisk together the all-purpose gluten-free flour, multigrain flour blend, xanthan gum (if using), and salt.
4. To the flour mixture, add the olive oil, eggs, cider vinegar, and the yeast mixture. Stir thoroughly until the dough is evenly hydrated. It should resemble thick, sticky batter rather than bread dough.
5. Grease a 9x5-inch loaf pan and line the bottom with parchment paper (optional).
6. Scoop the dough into the prepared pan and use a spatula to smooth the top.
7. Cover the pan loosely with a clean towel or wrap and let it rise in a warm, draft-free place for 1 hour or until the dough has nearly reached the top of the pan.
8. Preheat your oven to 375°F (or 190°C) while the dough is rising.
9. Once the dough has risen, bake it in the preheated oven for about 35-40 minutes or until the crust is golden and a thermometer inserted into the center of the loaf reads 200°F (or 93°C).
10. Remove the pan from the oven and let it cool on a wire rack for about 10 minutes. After it's cooled slightly, remove the bread from the pan and let it cool completely on the rack.
11. Slice the bread with a serrated knife once fully cooled. Enjoy your homemade gluten-free multigrain bread!

OATMEAL BREAD

Preparation Time: 15 minutes
Cooking Time: 45 minutes

INGREDIENTS:
- 4 cups of gluten-free oats
- 1 1/2 cups of warm water
- 2 teaspoons of active dry yeast
- 2 tablespoons of brown sugar
- 1 tablespoon of olive oil

- 2 eggs
- 1 teaspoon of salt
- 1 tablespoon of xanthan gum
- 1 tablespoon of apple cider vinegar

INSTRUCTIONS:
1. Preheat your oven to 375°F (190°C) and grease a loaf pan.
2. Take 2 cups of oats and blend them in a blender to make a smooth oat flour.
3. Pour the warm water into a large bowl and sprinkle the yeast into it. Let it sit for a couple of minutes till it gets frothy.
4. Stir in the sugar, olive oil, eggs, salt, and apple cider vinegar, ensuring they're thoroughly mixed.
5. Gradually add the oat flour and xanthan gum and mix until the mixture forms a sticky dough.
6. Pour the dough into the prepared loaf pan, covering it with a clean dishtowel. Let it rise in a warm place for about 30 minutes, or until the dough has roughly doubled in size.
7. Bake in the preheated oven for about 45 minutes, or until the top is golden brown.
8. Let the bread cool in the pan for about 10 minutes, then remove from the pan and transfer to a wire rack to cool completely.

QUINOA BREAD

Preparation Time: 20 minutes
Cooking Time: 90 minutes

INGREDIENTS:
- 1 cup of uncooked quinoa
- 1 cup of gluten-free oats
- 4 large eggs
- 1/4 cup of olive oil
- 1/2 cup of almond milk
- 3 tablespoons of honey
- 1 teaspoon of apple cider vinegar
- 1/2 teaspoon of sea salt
- 1 teaspoon of baking powder
- 1 teaspoon of baking soda
- Chia seeds or sesame seeds (optional, for topping)

INSTRUCTIONS:

1. Preheat your oven to 325°F. Grease a standard loaf pan and line it with parchment paper for easy removal.
2. In a large bowl, soak the quinoa and oats in water for about 15 minutes. After soaking, rinse and drain well.
3. Transfer the drained quinoa and oats into a food processor. Now, add eggs, honey, olive oil, almond milk, and apple cider vinegar. Blend until the mixture is smooth and creamy.
4. In a separate small bowl, combine salt, baking soda, and baking powder.
5. Pour these dry ingredients into the food processor and mix until well combined.
6. Pour the batter into the prepared loaf pan.
7. If desired, sprinkle the top of the batter with chia seeds or sesame seeds.
8. Bake in the oven for about 90 minutes, or until a toothpick inserted in the center comes out clean.
9. Let the bread cool completely in the pan before slicing.

SORGHUM BREAD

Preparation Time: 20 minutes
Cooking Time: 45 minutes

INGREDIENTS:
- 3 1/2 cups of gluten-free sorghum flour
- 1 1/2 cups of water (room temperature)
- 2 tablespoons of olive oil
- 3 tablespoons of honey
- 2 tablespoons of apple cider vinegar
- 1 1/2 teaspoons of sea salt
- 1/2 cup of tapioca starch
- 2 1/4 teaspoons of xanthan gum
- 2 1/4 teaspoons of active dry yeast

INSTRUCTIONS:
1. Mix together the dry ingredients (sorghum flour, tapioca starch, xanthan gum, salt, and yeast) in a large bowl.
2. In a separate bowl, combine the wet ingredients (water, olive oil, apple cider vinegar, honey) and mix them well.
3. Gradually add the wet ingredients into the dry ingredients and stir until the dough is smooth.
4. Grease a loaf pan lightly with olive oil or an alternative and distribute the dough evenly in the pan.

5. Cover the pan with a clean kitchen towel and set it in a warm spot. Let it rise for approximately 1 hour.
6. Preheat the oven to 375°F (190°C).
7. Once your loaf has risen, place it in the preheated oven and bake for 45 minutes or until the bread has a nice golden color on top.
8. Remove the bread from the oven and allow it to cool before slicing.

TEFF BREAD

Preparation Time: 15 minutes
Cooking Time: 40 minutes

INGREDIENTS:
- 2 cups of teff flour
- 1 cup of rice flour
- 1/2 cup of cornstarch
- 1 teaspoon of xanthan gum
- 1 tablespoon of baking powder
- 1 teaspoon of salt
- 1 1/2 cups of warm water
- 1/4 cup of olive oil
- 1 tablespoon of honey
- 2 large eggs
- 1 tablespoon of apple cider vinegar

INSTRUCTIONS:
1. Preheat your oven to 375 degrees F (190 degrees C). Grease a 9x5 inch loaf pan.
2. In a large bowl, combine the teff flour, rice flour, cornstarch, xanthan gum, baking powder, and salt.
3. In another bowl, mix the warm water, olive oil, honey, eggs, and apple cider vinegar.
4. Gradually add the wet ingredients to the dry ingredients, stirring until the mixture is smooth and well combined.
5. Pour the batter into the prepared loaf pan, smoothing the top with a spatula.
6. Bake in the preheated oven for about 40 minutes, or until a toothpick inserted into the center comes out clean.
7. Allow the bread to cool in the pan for 10 minutes, then transfer it to a wire rack to cool completely before slicing.
8. Enjoy your gluten-free teff bread with your favorite spreads, or simply as is!

HIGH-FIBER LOAVES, ROLLS, AND BUNS

APPLE CINNAMON BREAD

Preparation Time: 20 minutes
Cooking Time: 50 minutes

INGREDIENTS:
For the bread:
- 2 cups of gluten-free all-purpose flour
- 1 1/2 teaspoons of xanthan gum (only if your flour blend doesn't already include it)
- 1 cup of granulated sugar
- 2 teaspoons of ground cinnamon
- 1 teaspoon of baking powder
- 1/2 teaspoon of baking soda
- 1/2 teaspoon of salt
- 1 cup of unsweetened applesauce
- 3/4 cup of vegetable oil
- 4 large eggs
- 11 cups of peeled and finely diced apple

For the topping:
- 2 tablespoons of granulated sugar
- 1/2 teaspoon of ground cinnamon

INSTRUCTIONS:
1. Preheat your oven to 350°F (175°C) and grease a 9x5 inch loaf pan, then sprinkle with a bit of gluten-free flour.
2. In a large mixing bowl, combine the flour, xanthan gum (if using), sugar, cinnamon, baking powder, baking soda, and salt.
3. In a separate bowl, mix the applesauce, vegetable oil, and eggs until well combined.
4. Gradually add the dry ingredients to the wet mixture, stirring until just combined.
5. Fold in the finely diced apple
6. Pour the batter into your prepped loaf pan, spreading it out evenly with a spatula.
7. For the topping, mix the sugar and cinnamon in a small bowl.
8. Sprinkle the cinnamon-sugar mixture evenly over the top of the batter.
9. Bake in the preheated oven for 50-55 minutes, or until a toothpick inserted into the center of the bread comes out clean.
10. Allow the bread to cool in the pan for about 10 minutes, then remove from pan and transfer to a wire rack to cool completely.

HIGH-FIBER BREAKFAST BREAD

Preparation Time: 20 minutes
Cooking Time: 60 minutes

INGREDIENTS:
- 2 cups of gluten-free all-purpose flour
- 1 cup of almond flour
- 1 cup of rolled oats (ensure they are certified gluten-free)
- 2 tablespoons of chia seeds
- 2 tablespoons of flax seeds
- 1/4 cup of psyllium husk powder
- 1/2 cup of raisins or dried fruit of choice (optional)
- 1/2 cup of chopped nuts (optional)
- 2 teaspoons of baking powder (make sure it's gluten-free)
- 1/2 teaspoon of salt
- 2 large eggs
- 1 1/2 cups of non-dairy milk
- 1/4 cup of coconut oil
- 1/4 cup of honey or maple syrup

INSTRUCTIONS:
1. Preheat your oven to 350°F (175°C) and grease a loaf pan.
2. In a large bowl, combine the gluten-free all-purpose flour, almond flour, gluten-free rolled oats, chia seeds, flax seeds, psyllium husk powder, baking powder, salt, dried fruit, and nuts if using. Mix until well combined.
3. In a separate bowl, whisk together the eggs, non-dairy milk, coconut oil, and honey or maple syrup.
4. Gradually pour the wet mixture into the dry ingredients, stirring until the mixture forms a sticky, thick dough. Let sit for about 5 minutes to allow the fibers to absorb the liquid.
5. Transfer the dough into the greased loaf pan, pressing it down with the back of a spoon to even out the top.
6. Bake for approximately 60 minutes. The bread should be golden brown, and a toothpick inserted into the middle should come out clean.
7. Remove from oven and let cool in the pan for about 10 minutes before transferring to a wire rack to cool completely.
8. Slice and enjoy with your favorite toppings.

CHIA SEED BREAD

Preparation Time: 15 minutes
Cooking Time: 60 minutes

INGREDIENTS:
- 2 cups of gluten-free flour
- 1/2 cup of chia seeds
- 1/2 cup of sunflower seeds
- 2 teaspoons of baking powder
- 1 teaspoon of fine sea salt
- 5 eggs
- 1/4 cup of coconut oil, melted and cooled
- 2 tablespoons of honey
- 1/4 cup of water
- 1/4 cup of apple cider vinegar

INSTRUCTIONS:
1. Preheat the oven to 325°F and line a loaf pan with parchment paper or lightly grease it.
2. In a large mixing bowl, combine the gluten-free flour, chia seeds, sunflower seeds, baking powder, and sea salt.
3. In a separate bowl, beat the eggs. Then add the melted coconut oil, honey, water, and apple cider vinegar. Mix until well combined.
4. Slowly add the dry ingredients into the wet mixture, stirring constantly to avoid lumps.
5. Pour the batter into the prepared loaf pan and smooth the top with a spatula.
6. Bake in the preheated oven for 60 minutes, or until a toothpick inserted into the center comes out clean.
7. Remove the bread from the oven and let it cool in the pan for 10 minutes. Then transfer it to a wire rack to cool completely.
8. Slice and enjoy your gluten-free chia seed bread as is or toast it for a crunchy treat!

FIBER-RICH ZUCCHINI BREAD

Preparation Time: 15 minutes
Cooking Time: 60 minutes

INGREDIENTS:
- 1 1/2 cups of gluten-free flour

- 1 teaspoon of xanthan gum (skip if your flour blend already includes it)
- 1/2 cup of ground flaxseed meal
- 1 teaspoon of baking powder
- 1/2 teaspoon of baking soda
- 1/2 teaspoon of salt
- 1/2 teaspoon of ground cinnamon
- 1/4 teaspoon of ground nutmeg
- 2 medium-sized zucchinis, shredded (about 2 cups)
- 1/2 cup of unsweetened applesauce
- 1/2 cup of honey or maple syrup
- 2 large eggs, at room temperature
- 1/4 cup of coconut oil, melted
- 1 teaspoon of pure vanilla extract
- 1/2 cup of walnuts, chopped

INSTRUCTIONS:
1. Preheat your oven to 350°F (175°C). Lightly grease a loaf pan and set it aside.
2. In a large mixing bowl, combine the gluten-free flour, xanthan gum (if using), flaxseed meal, baking powder, baking soda, salt, cinnamon, and nutmeg. Stir until well mixed.
3. Take the shredded zucchini and squeeze it between paper towels to remove excess moisture.
4. In another bowl, combine the applesauce, honey/maple syrup, eggs, coconut oil, and vanilla extract. Mix until well blended.
5. Gradually add the dry ingredients to the wet ingredients while stirring. Mix until fully combined.
6. Stir in the shredded zucchini and chopped walnuts.
7. Pour the batter into the prepared loaf pan.
8. Bake for 60 minutes or until a toothpick inserted in the center comes out clean.
9. Allow it to cool in the pan for 10 minutes, then remove the bread from the pan and let cool completely on a wire rack.
10. Slice and enjoy your gluten-free fiber-rich zucchini bread!

FLAX AND OAT ROLLS

Preparation Time: 15 minutes
Cooking Time: 25 minutes

INGREDIENTS:
- 2 cups gluten-free oat flour

- 1/2 cup whole flax seeds
- 2 tsp baking powder (ensure gluten-free)
- 1/2 tsp salt
- 2 large eggs
- 1/4 cup coconut oil, melted
- 1 cup almond milk
- 2 tbsp honey or maple syrup for sweetness

INSTRUCTIONS:
1. Preheat your oven to 375°F (190°C) with the rack in the middle position.
2. In a large bowl, combine the oat flour, flax seeds, baking powder, and salt. Mix well till combined.
3. In another bowl, whisk together the eggs, melted coconut oil, almond milk, and honey or maple syrup until the mixture is smooth and well combined.
4. Gradually add the wet ingredients into the dry ingredients, stirring well to make sure there are no lumps. The dough should be sticky and a little bit elastic.
5. Line a baking sheet with parchment paper or lightly grease it with oil. Using a spoon, scoop out the mixture and shape it into rolls. You should be able to make approximately 12 rolls.
6. Place the rolls on the prepared baking sheet, leaving enough space in between each for them to expand.
7. Bake for about 25 minutes, or until the rolls are golden brown and a toothpick inserted in the center comes out clean.
8. Once done, remove from the oven and let the rolls cool on the baking sheet before serving. Enjoy these delicious gluten-free flax and oat rolls fresh from the oven with your choice of spread!

FLAXSEED BREAD

Preparation Time: 15 minutes
Cooking Time: 45 minutes

INGREDIENTS:
- 2 cups almond flour
- 1 cup ground flaxseed
- 4 large eggs
- 2 tablespoons honey
- 1/2 teaspoon baking soda
- 1 teaspoon apple cider vinegar
- 1/4 teaspoon salt

- Sprinkling of sesame seeds (optional)

INSTRUCTIONS:
1. Preheat the oven to 350°F (175°C). Lightly grease a loaf tin and line with parchment paper.
2. In a large bowl, combine the almond flour, ground flaxseed, and salt.
3. In another bowl, whisk together the eggs and honey until smooth.
4. Add the baking soda and apple cider vinegar to the egg mixture, ensuring it fully reacts.
5. Gradually add the dry ingredients to the egg mixture and stir until you have a smooth dough.
6. Pour the dough into the previously prepared loaf tin and spread evenly with a spatula.
7. Optional: Sprinkle the top with a liberal amount of sesame seeds for added crunch and texture.
8. Bake in the preheated oven for around 45 minutes or until the top is golden brown and a skewer inserted into the center comes out clean.
9. Allow the bread to cool in the tin for about 20 minutes, then carefully remove from the tin and let it cool completely on a wire rack.
10. Slice the bread and serve with your favorite spread or use it for sandwiches. Enjoy your gluten-free flaxseed bread!
11. Remember to store in an airtight container and consume within a few days for best freshness.

GREEN PEA & OAT BREAD

Preparation Time: 20 minutes
Cooking Time: 45 minutes

INGREDIENTS:
- 3 cups of gluten-free oats
- 2 cups of green pea flour
- 1 cup of warm water
- 2 tablespoons of honey
- 1 sachet (about 2 teaspoons) of active dry yeast
- 2 tablespoons of olive oil
- 1 teaspoon of salt
- 1/2 teaspoon of baking powder
- 1/2 cup of unsweetened almond milk (or any dairy-free substitute)

INSTRUCTIONS:
1. Start by preheating your oven to 375°F (190°C) and preparing a loaf pan by greasing it.
2. In a large bowl, combine 2 cups of gluten-free oats and green pea flour.
3. Dissolve honey in the cup of warm water. Add the active dry yeast to this mixture and let it sit for about 5 minutes, or until it froths.
4. Pour the yeast mixture into the bowl with the oats and green pea flour. Mix well to combine.
5. Add the olive oil, salt, and baking powder to the mixture. Stir well until all ingredients are integrated.
6. Gradually pour in the almond milk, continuously stirring until a dough is formed.
7. Transfer the dough into the prepared loaf pan evenly and smooth out the top with a spatula.
8. Sprinkle the top with the remaining 1 cup of oats.
9. Bake for approximately 45 minutes, or until the top is golden brown and a toothpick inserted into the center comes out clean.
10. Remove from the oven and allow it to cool before slicing.
11. Serve it plain, with butter, jam, or any desired spread.

HIGH-FIBER BURGER BUNS

Preparation Time: 20 minutes
Cooking Time: 25 minutes

INGREDIENTS:
- 2 cups of gluten-free all-purpose flour
- 1 cup of almond meal
- 1/2 cup of flaxseed meal
- 1 tablespoon of baking powder
- 1/2 teaspoon of salt
- 3 large eggs
- 3/4 cup of water
- 1/4 cup of extra virgin olive oil
- 1 tablespoon of apple cider vinegar
- Sesame seeds or poppy seeds for topping (optional)

INSTRUCTIONS:
1. Preheat the oven to 350°F (175°C) and line a baking sheet with parchment paper.
2. In a large bowl, combine the gluten-free all-purpose flour, almond meal, flaxseed meal, baking powder, and salt. Stir with a whisk until well combined.

3. In a separate bowl, whisk together the eggs, water, olive oil, and apple cider vinegar.
4. Pour the wet ingredients into the dry ingredients and stir until well combined.
5. Let the dough sit for 5 minutes to allow the flaxseed to absorb some of the liquid.
6. With wet hands, form the dough into 6 equal bun shapes and place them on the prepared baking sheet.
7. If desired, sprinkle the tops with sesame seeds or poppy seeds.
8. Bake the buns for 25-30 minutes, or until they are golden brown and firm to the touch.
9. Let the buns cool on the baking sheet for 5 minutes, then transfer to a wire rack to cool completely.
10. Serve these high-fiber, gluten-free burger buns with your favorite burger toppings and enjoy!

HIGH-FIBER SANDWICH BREAD

Preparation Time: 15 minutes
Cooking Time: 40 minutes

INGREDIENTS:
- 1 1/2 cups of warm water
- 1 tablespoon of quick-rise yeast
- 3 tablespoons of brown sugar
- 2 tablespoons of olive oil
- 2 cups of gluten-free flour
- 1 cup of brown rice flour
- 1 cup of oat flour
- 1 cup of flaxseed meal
- 1/2 cup of psyllium husk powder
- 1 1/2 teaspoons of sea salt
- 3 eggs

INSTRUCTIONS:
1. Preheat your oven to 375°F (190°C) and lightly oil a bread pan.
2. In a large bowl, combine the warm water, quick-rise yeast, and brown sugar. Allow the mixture to sit for a few minutes until frothy.
3. Add in the olive oil, followed by the gluten-free flour, brown rice flour, oat flour, flaxseed meal, psyllium husk powder and sea salt. Mix until everything is well combined.
4. Whisk the eggs in a separate bowl before adding to the mixture. Stir until the dough begins to pull away from the sides.

5. Scrape the dough into the greased bread pan. Cover with a clean kitchen towel and let it rise in a warm location for about 30 to 45 minutes. The dough should be about an inch above the edge of the bread pan.
6. Once risen, place your bread pan in the preheated oven and bake for approximately 35 to 40 minutes. The bread should have a golden-brown crust and sound hollow when tapped on the bottom.
7. Remove the bread from the oven and let cool in the pan for a few minutes, then transfer onto a wire rack to cool completely.
8. Once cooled, slice and enjoy your gluten-free high-fiber sandwich bread.

MULTIGRAIN ROLLS

Preparation Time: 15 minutes
Cooking Time: 25 minutes

INGREDIENTS:
- 2 cups of gluten-free multigrain bread mix
- 1 tablespoon of active dry yeast
- 2 tablespoons of granulated sugar
- 1 1/4 cup of warm water (110 to 115 degrees F)
- 1 large egg, beaten
- 2 tablespoons of unsalted butter, melted
- 1 teaspoon of cider vinegar
- 1/4 teaspoon of salt
- Cornmeal for dusting
- Optional: 1 tablespoon of mixed seeds (flax, sunflower, and sesame) for topping

INSTRUCTIONS:
1. In a large bowl, combine the gluten-free bread mix, yeast, and sugar. Stir until well mixed.
2. Add the warm water to the dry ingredients and stir until combined. Then, add the beaten egg, melted butter, apple cider vinegar, and salt. Stir until the dough is smooth.
3. Cover the bowl with a clean kitchen towel and let rise in a warm place for 1 hour, or until doubled in its size.
4. Preheat the oven to 375 degrees F. Line a baking sheet with parchment paper and sprinkle with cornmeal.
5. Once the dough has risen, divide it into 12 equal parts. Form each piece into a ball and place it on the prepared baking sheet.

6. If you wish, you can brush the tops of the rolls with a bit of water and sprinkle them with the mixed seeds.
7. Bake the rolls in the preheated oven for 20-25 minutes, or until they are golden brown and sound hollow when you tap the bottom of the roll.
8. Remove the rolls from the oven and let them cool on the baking sheet for 5 minutes, then move them to a wire rack to cool completely before serving.

OAT BRAN BREAD

Preparation Time: 15 minutes
Cooking Time: 45 minutes

INGREDIENTS:
- 2 cups of gluten-free oat bran
- 1 cup of gluten-free all-purpose flour
- 1 teaspoon of baking powder
- 1 teaspoon of baking soda
- 1/2 teaspoon of salt
- 1 cup of unsweetened applesauce
- 3 large eggs
- 1/4 cup of honey
- 1/4 cup of coconut oil, melted
- 1 teaspoon of pure vanilla extract

INSTRUCTIONS:
1. Start by preheating your oven to 375°F (190°C), and greasing a loaf pan with some coconut oil.
2. In a large mixing bowl, combine the oat bran, gluten-free all-purpose flour, baking powder, baking soda, and salt.
3. In a separate bowl, combine the unsweetened applesauce, eggs, honey, melted coconut oil, and vanilla extract.
4. Gradually mix the wet ingredients into the dry until everything is fully incorporated.
5. Pour the bread batter into the pre-greased loaf pan, making sure to spread it out evenly.
6. Place the loaf pan in the preheated oven and bake for about 45 minutes, or until a toothpick inserted in the middle of the bread comes out clean.
7. Once done, remove the bread from the oven and let it cool in the pan for about 10 minutes before transferring it to a wire rack to cool completely.
8. Slice the bread and serve it warm with some butter or jam.

PSYLLIUM HUSK BREAD

Preparation Time: 15 minutes
Cooking Time: 75 minutes

INGREDIENTS:
- 1 1/4 cup of warm water
- 2 tablespoons of maple syrup
- 1 packet (or 2 1/4 teaspoons) of active dry yeast
- 1 cup of almond flour
- 1 cup of oat flour
- 1/2 cup of ground flaxseeds
- 1/2 cup of psyllium husk powder
- 2 tablespoons of apple cider vinegar
- 4 eggs
- 1/2 teaspoon of sea salt

INSTRUCTIONS:
1. Start by combining the warm water and maple syrup in a large bowl, then add the active dry yeast. Let this mixture sit for a few minutes to activate the yeast.
2. In a separate bowl, combine the almond flour, oat flour, ground flaxseeds, psyllium husk powder, and sea salt. Stir these dry ingredients together until they are fully combined.
3. Now add the apple cider vinegar and eggs to the yeast mixture. Stir until it's well mixed.
4. Gradually add the dry ingredients to the wet mixture, making sure to stir well after each addition to prevent any lumps from forming.
5. Once all the dry ingredients have been added, continue to stir the mix until a sticky dough forms.
6. Preheat your oven to 350°F and line a 9x5-inch loaf pan with parchment paper.
7. Transfer the dough into the lined loaf pan. Smooth the top with a spatula and let it rise in a warm place for about 15 minutes.
8. Bake the bread in the preheated oven for about 60 minutes or until the top of the bread has browned and a toothpick inserted into the center comes out clean.
9. Let the bread cool in the pan for 10 minutes, then transfer it to a wire rack to cool completely.
10. Slice your gluten-free psyllium husk bread and enjoy plain or toasted with your favorite spread.

SWEET POTATO BREAD

Preparation Time: 20 minutes
Cooking Time: 60 minutes

INGREDIENTS:
- 1 cup mashed sweet potato
- 2 large eggs
- 1/2 cup melted coconut oil
- 1/4 cup maple syrup
- 1 cup almond flour
- 1/2 cup coconut flour
- 1 teaspoon baking soda
- 1/2 teaspoon salt
- 1 teaspoon ground cinnamon
- 1/2 teaspoon ground nutmeg
- 1/4 teaspoon ground ginger

INSTRUCTIONS:
1. Preheat your oven to 350°F (175°C). Grease a 9x5 inch loaf pan or line it with parchment paper.
2. In a large mixing bowl, combine the mashed sweet potato, eggs, melted coconut oil, and maple syrup. Mix until well incorporated.
3. In another bowl, mix the almond flour, coconut flour, baking soda, salt, cinnamon, nutmeg, and ginger.
4. Gradually add the dry ingredients to the wet ingredients, mixing continuously until the batter is smooth.
5. Pour the batter into the prepared loaf pan and smooth the top with a spatula.
6. Bake for approximately 60 minutes, or until a toothpick inserted in the center comes out clean.
7. Remove the bread from the oven and let it cool in the pan for 10-15 minutes. Afterward, transfer it to a wire rack to cool completely.
8. Slice and serve the bread warm! Enjoy it on its own or with your favorite spread.

SEEDED WHOLE GRAIN BREAD

Preparation Time: 20 minutes
Cooking Time: 40 minutes

INGREDIENTS:

- 1 1/2 cups of warm water
- 1 tablespoon of sugar
- 2 teaspoons of dry instant yeast
- 3 cups of gluten-free whole grain flour mix
- 1 1/2 teaspoons of salt
- 2 tablespoons of olive oil
- 2 tablespoons of honey
- 1/4 cup of mixed seeds (optional: sunflower, flax, pumpkin)
- 1 tablespoon of egg white (optional, for topping)

INSTRUCTIONS:
1. In a small bowl, dissolve the sugar into the warm water. Then, add the yeast and let it sit for about 5 minutes, or until it becomes foamy.
2. In a large mixing bowl, combine the gluten-free whole grain flour mix and salt.
3. Make a well in the center of the flour and pour in the yeast mixture, olive oil, and honey. Stir until the mixture forms a sticky dough.
4. Add the mixed seeds into the dough and stir until they are evenly distributed.
5. Transfer the dough to a greased loaf pan and smooth the top with a spatula. If you're using the egg white for topping, brush it over the dough's surface and sprinkle with additional seeds, if desired.
6. Cover the pan with a clean towel and let the dough rise in a warm area for around 30-60 minutes or until it has nearly doubled in size.
7. Preheat your oven to 375°F (190°C).
8. Bake the bread in the preheated oven for 35-40 minutes, or until the top is golden and a toothpick inserted into the middle comes out clean.
9. Allow the bread to cool in the pan for about 10 minutes, then transfer it to a wire rack to cool completely before slicing and serving.

WHOLE GRAIN DINNER ROLLS

Preparation Time: 30 minutes
Cooking Time: 25 minutes

INGREDIENTS:
- 1 cup of warm water
- 2 tablespoons of white sugar
- 1 packet (2 1/4 teaspoons) of active dry yeast
- 2 cups of gluten-free flour blend (make sure the blend already contains xanthan gum)
- 1 cup of whole grain gluten-free flour

- 1/2 teaspoon of salt
- 1/4 cup of olive oil
- 2 large eggs
- 1 teaspoon of apple cider vinegar

INSTRUCTIONS:
1. In a small bowl, mix the warm water and sugar until sugar is dissolved. Add the yeast to the mixture and let it sit for 5 minutes or until it's frothy.
2. Meanwhile, in a large mixing bowl, combine the gluten-free flour blend, whole grain gluten-free flour, and salt. Mix until well combined.
3. In a separate bowl, beat the eggs, apple cider vinegar, and olive oil together, then pour these wet ingredients into the dry flour mixture.
4. Add the yeast mixture into the flour mixture. Stir until everything is well incorporated. The dough will be sticky, so don't worry if it's not as firm as regular dough.
5. Cover the bowl with a clean dish towel and let it sit in a warm spot for about an hour or until it doubles in size.
6. Preheat your oven to 375°F. Line a baking sheet with parchment paper.
7. With oiled hands, take golf ball-sized portions of the dough and roll them into balls. Place each ball on the lined baking sheet.
8. Let the dough balls rest for 10 minutes, then bake for 20-25 minutes until they are golden brown.
9. Allow the rolls to cool before serving.

SOURDOUGH LOAVES AND BAGUETTES

CARAMELIZED ONION SOURDOUGH BAGUETTE

Preparation Time: 45 minutes
Cooking Time: 25 minutes

INGREDIENTS:
For the dough:
- 3 cups of gluten-free flour
- 2 teaspoons of xanthan gum (if your gluten-free flour blend doesn't already contain it)
- 1 sachet (about 2 teaspoons) of dried yeast
- 1 1/2 teaspoons of sea salt
- 1 1/4 cup of lukewarm water
- 2 tablespoons of olive oil

For the onion filling:
- 2 medium red onions, sliced
- 2 tablespoons of olive oil
- 2 tablespoons of balsamic vinegar
- 1 tablespoon of brown sugar
- A pinch of sea salt
- 1/2 cup grated parmesan cheese (optional)

INSTRUCTIONS:
1. In a large bowl, combine the gluten-free flour, xanthan gum, yeast, and salt. Stir until the ingredients are evenly distributed.
2. Gradually add the lukewarm water and olive oil while stirring continuously. A sticky dough will form.
3. Place the dough on a lightly floured surface and knead it for 5 minutes. If the dough is too sticky, you can add a little more flour.
4. Shape the dough into a baguette shape and place it on a baking sheet lined with parchment paper. Cover the dough with a clean kitchen towel and let it rise in a warm place for about 2 hours.
5. While the dough is rising, prepare the caramelized onions. Heat the olive oil in a pan over medium heat, add the onions and cook for about 10 minutes, or until the onions are soft and translucent.
6. Add the balsamic vinegar, brown sugar, and a pinch of salt to the onions. Stir and cook for another 10 minutes, or until the onions are caramelized.
7. Preheat the oven to 425°F (220°C).

8. After the dough has risen, use a sharp knife to make diagonal slashes along the top of the baguette.
9. Bake the baguette for 10 minutes, then remove it from the oven and top it with the caramelized onions and grated parmesan cheese (if using).
10. Return the baguette to the oven and bake for an additional 15 minutes, or until the baguette is golden and the cheese is melted.

CARAMELIZED ONION AND GRUYÈRE SOURDOUGH BAGUETTE

Preparation Time: 60 minutes
Cooking Time: 30 minutes

INGREDIENTS:
For the baguette:
- 1 1/2 cups of warm water
- 2 1/4 teaspoons of active yeast
- 1 tablespoon of granulated sugar
- 3 cups of gluten-free flour blend
- 1 teaspoon of xanthan gum (skip if your flour blend has it)
- 1 teaspoon of salt

For the filling:
- 2 tablespoons of butter
- 2 large onions, thinly sliced
- 1 teaspoon of sugar
- 1/2 teaspoon of salt
- 1/2 teaspoon of black pepper
- 1 cup of Gruyere cheese, grated

INSTRUCTIONS:
- Stir together warm water, active yeast, and granulated sugar in a large bowl. Let it sit for 10 minutes.
- In another bowl, mix the gluten-free flour blend, xanthan gum, and salt.
- Slowly mix the dry ingredients into the wet until you form a unified dough. If the dough is too sticky, add a bit more flour.
- Cover the bowl with a cloth and let it rise in a warm place for about 1 hour.
- Preheat your oven to 425°F (220°C) and line a baking sheet with parchment paper.
- While the dough is rising, heat the butter in a pan over medium heat. Add the onions, sugar, salt, and pepper and cook for 15 to 20 minutes or until the onions are caramelized and browned.

- Once the dough has risen, turn it out onto a floured surface and divide it into two parts. Roll each part into a log shape and place them on the prepared baking sheet.
- Slice the top of the loaves diagonally with a knife, about 1/2 an inch deep.
- Scoop the caramelized onion evenly into the cuts, pressing it down gently.
- Sprinkle the Gruyere cheese on top of the onions.
- Bake the baguettes in the preheated oven for 25 to 30 minutes until they become a golden-brown color.
- Let it cool for a bit before serving.

CARAMELIZED ONION & THYME SOURDOUGH LOAF

Preparation Time: 90 minutes
Cooking Time: 45 minutes

INGREDIENTS:
For the caramelized onions:
- 2 large onions, thinly sliced
- 2 tablespoons of olive oil
- 1 teaspoon of balsamic vinegar
- 1 teaspoon of sugar
- 1/2 teaspoon of dried thyme

For the bread:
- 1 cup of gluten-free sourdough starter
- 2 cups of gluten-free flour blend
- 1 cup of warm water
- 1 teaspoon of salt
- 1 tablespoon of dried thyme
- Olive oil for brushing

INSTRUCTIONS:
1. Begin by making the caramelized onions. Heat the olive oil over medium heat in a large skillet. Add the onions, balsamic vinegar, sugar, and dried thyme. Cook, stirring often, until onions are soft and caramelized, which should take roughly 30 minutes.
2. While the onions are cooking, in a large bowl, combine the gluten-free sourdough starter, gluten-free flour blend, warm water, salt, and dried thyme.
3. Once the onions have finished cooking, let them cool, then add them to the bread mixture. Mix thoroughly to combine.

4. Cover the bowl with a tea towel and set aside in a warm location for approximately one hour or until the bread dough has doubled in size.
5. Preheat your oven to 450 degrees F (232 degrees C) and place a Dutch oven with its lid on into the oven to preheat.
6. Once the dough has risen, shape it into a round loaf (be careful because it will be sticky). Brush the top with olive oil.
7. Carefully take the preheated Dutch oven out and place the loaf into it, then replace the lid and put it back into the oven.
8. Bake for 30 minutes with the lid on, then remove the lid and bake for an additional 15 minutes, or until the loaf has a golden-brown crust.
9. Once it's done, let the loaf cool before slicing and serving.

CHEDDAR & CHIVE GLUTEN-FREE SOURDOUGH BAGUETTE

Preparation Time: 20 minutes
Cooking Time: 45 minutes

INGREDIENTS:
- 1 cup of gluten-free sourdough starter
- 1 cup of warm water
- 1 tablespoon of sugar
- 1 1/2 cups of gluten-free all-purpose flour
- 2 teaspoons of xanthan gum (omit if your flour blend already contains it)
- 1 teaspoon of salt
- 1 tablespoon of olive oil
- 1 cup of sharp cheddar cheese, shredded
- 1/4 cup of fresh chives, finely chopped

INSTRUCTIONS:
1. In a large mixing bowl, combine the sourdough starter, warm water, and sugar. Stir until the sugar is fully dissolved.
2. In a separate bowl, mix the gluten-free flour, xanthan gum (if using), and salt.
3. Gradually add the flour mixture to the sourdough starter mixture, stirring continually until the ingredients are thoroughly combined.
4. Knead the dough in the bowl for about 5 minutes, then gradually add the olive oil, continuing to knead until the dough is smooth and elastic.
5. Add the shredded cheddar cheese and finely chopped chives to the dough, folding until they're evenly distributed throughout the dough.
6. Cover the dough with a damp cloth and let it rise in a warm place for about 2 hours, or until it has roughly doubled in size.

7. Preheat your oven to 450°F (232°C) and line a baking sheet with parchment paper.
8. Shape the dough into a long, thin baguette shape, place it on the lined baking sheet, and let it rest for about 10 minutes.
9. Using a serrated knife, make a series of diagonal slashes along the top of the baguette.
10. Bake the baguette in the preheated oven for approximately 45 minutes, or until it's golden brown and sounds hollow when tapped on the bottom.
11. Let the baguette cool on a wire rack before slicing and serving.

CHEDDAR & JALAPEÑO SOURDOUGH BAGUETTE

Preparation Time: 20 minutes
Cooking Time: 35 minutes

INGREDIENTS:
- 1 1/2 cups of gluten-free flour
- 1 teaspoon of xanthan gum (only if your gluten-free flour blend doesn't have it)
- 1/2 teaspoon salt
- 1 cup of sourdough starter (gluten-free)
- 1 tablespoon of warmed honey
- 1 1/2 teaspoons of active dry yeast
- 1 tablespoon of olive oil
- 1 jalapeño, finely chopped
- 1 cup of shredded cheddar cheese
- 1/2 cup of warm water
- Cornmeal, for dusting
- Egg wash for brushing

INSTRUCTIONS:
1. In a large mixing bowl, combine the gluten-free flour, xanthan gum (if needed), and salt.
2. In another bowl, stir the warm water, warmed honey, and active dry yeast. Let it sit until it becomes foamy, around 5-10 minutes.
3. Pour the yeasty mixture, sourdough starter, and olive oil into the dry ingredients. Use an electric mixer and blend until the mixture is smooth.
4. Fold in the finely chopped jalapeño and shredded cheddar cheese.
5. Scrape the sticky dough into a greased and cornmeal-dusted baguette pan.
6. Cover with a kitchen towel and let it rise in a warm place until it becomes double in size. This should take about an hour.
7. Preheat the oven to 400° F.

8. Brush the risen dough with the egg wash to give the crust a golden color.

9. Bake for 35 minutes, or until the top turns golden brown and sounds hollow when tapped.

10. Take out the pan from the oven and let it cool for a few minutes. Then, remove the cheddar & jalapeño sourdough baguette from the pan and allow it to cool further on a wire rack before slicing and serving.

11. Enjoy your flavorful, gluten-free homemade cheddar & jalapeño sourdough baguette, which is best when served while still warm.

CLASSIC GLUTEN-FREE SOURDOUGH LOAF

Preparation Time: 30 minutes
Cooking Time: 40 minutes

INGREDIENTS:
- 1 1/4 cup of warm water (around 110°F)
- 1 tablespoon of honey
- 2 1/4 teaspoons of active dry yeast
- 3 cups of gluten-free flour blend
- 2 teaspoons of xanthan gum (exclude if your flour blend already contains it)
- 1 1/4 teaspoons of salt
- 2 teaspoons of apple cider vinegar
- 2 egg whites
- 2 tablespoons of melted unsalted butter or olive oil
- 1/2 cup of gluten-free sourdough starter

INSTRUCTIONS:
1. Combine the warm water and honey in a small bowl and stir until the honey is dissolved. Sprinkle the yeast on top and set aside for about 5-10 minutes or until the yeast mixture is frothy.
2. In a large bowl, combine the gluten-free flour, xanthan gum, and salt. Mix well.
3. In another bowl, combine the apple cider vinegar, egg whites, melted butter or oil, and gluten-free sourdough starter. Stir well.
4. Pour in the yeast mixture, then the egg mixture into the dry ingredients. Mix until it forms a sticky dough, using a spoon or spatula.
5. Cover the bowl with a kitchen towel and let it rise in a warm place for about 2 hours, or until the dough has doubled in size.
6. Preheat your oven to 425°F.

7. Once the dough has risen, gently scoop it into a greased loaf pan and smooth the top with a wet spatula.
8. Place the loaf pan into the oven and bake for about 40 minutes, or until the top of the loaf is golden brown and a toothpick inserted into the center comes out clean.
9. Let the loaf cool in the pan for 10 minutes, then remove it from the pan and let it cool completely on a wire rack before slicing.

GARLIC & HERB SOURDOUGH LOAF

Preparation Time: 90 minutes
Cooking Time: 40 minutes

INGREDIENTS:
- 1 1/2 cups of gluten-free sourdough starter
- 1 tablespoon of honey
- 1 3/4 cups of gluten-free all-purpose flour
- 1 teaspoon of salt
- 1 cup of warm water
- 2 tablespoons of olive oil
- 3 cloves of garlic, minced
- 1 tablespoon of dried rosemary
- 1 tablespoon of dried thyme
- 1 tablespoon of dried basil

INSTRUCTIONS:
1. In a large bowl, combine your gluten-free sourdough starter, honey, gluten-free all-purpose flour, salt, and warm water. Mix the ingredients well until you have a smooth, sticky dough. This process should take around 5 minutes.
2. Add your minced garlic, dried herbs, and olive oil to the dough mixture. Knead the dough until these additions are fully integrated.
3. Cover the bowl loosely with plastic wrap or a damp cloth, set it in a warm spot, and let the dough rise for about an hour. Your dough should be visibly puffier at the end of this hour.
4. Preheat your oven to 450 degrees F. Place a Dutch oven with the lid on into the oven while it preheats.
5. Once the dough has risen and your oven is heated, transfer dough into the preheated Dutch oven. Ensure you handle the dough gently to maintain its form and texture.

6. Bake the loaf at 450 degrees F for 30 minutes with the lid on, and then remove the lid and continue baking for another 10 minutes, until the top of the loaf has a crisp, golden crust.
7. Remove the loaf from the oven and let it cool on a wire rack.
8. Enjoy your homemade gluten-free garlic & herb sourdough loaf!

GARLIC & THYME SOURDOUGH LOAF

Preparation Time: 25 minutes (plus overnight for sourdough starter)
Cooking Time: 45 minutes

INGREDIENTS:
- 2 cups gluten-free sourdough starter
- 3 1/2 cups gluten-free bread flour
- 1 1/4 cups water
- 2 teaspoons xanthan gum
- 1 tablespoon olive oil
- 1 1/2 teaspoons salt
- 2 garlic cloves, minced
- 2 teaspoons fresh thyme, finely chopped
- Cornmeal for dusting

INSTRUCTIONS:
1. In a large bowl, combine the sourdough starter, gluten-free bread flour, water, xanthan gum, olive oil, and salt. Mix until the dough comes together.
2. Knead the dough on a floured surface for about 10 minutes until it becomes smooth and elastic.
3. Place the dough back into the bowl, cover it with a clean kitchen cloth and let it rise at room temperature for about 3 to 4 hours or until it doubles in size.
4. Punch down the risen dough and turn it out onto a floured surface. Sprinkle the minced garlic and chopped thyme over the dough, fold the dough over a few times to incorporate the seasonings.
5. Shape the dough into a loaf and place it on a baking sheet dusted with cornmeal.
6. Cover the loaf with a clean kitchen cloth and let it rise again for about 1 to 2 hours or until it almost doubles in size.
7. Preheat the oven to 425°F and place a roasting pan filled with hot water in the bottom of the oven to create steam.
8. Slash the top of the loaf with a sharp knife to create a pattern.

9. Bake the loaf for 45 to 50 minutes or until golden brown and the bottom of the loaf sounds hollow when tapped. If the loaf is browning too quickly, you can cover it loosely with aluminum foil.
10. Remove from oven and let cool on a wire rack before slicing.

HERBES DE PROVENCE SOURDOUGH LOAF

Preparation Time: 20 minutes
Cooking Time: 40 minutes

INGREDIENTS:
- 3 cups of gluten-free bread flour
- 1 1/2 cups of lukewarm water
- 1 tablespoon of salt
- 1 tablespoon of sugar
- 2 tablespoons of herbs de Provence
- 1 tablespoon of active dry yeast
- 1/2 cup of gluten-free sourdough starter
- Olive oil for brushing the loaf

INSTRUCTIONS:
1. In a large bowl, combine the bread flour, salt, sugar, and herbs de Provence.
2. Dissolve the yeast in the lukewarm water and let it sit for about 5 minutes until it appears frothy. This confirms that your yeast is active.
3. Add the yeast mixture and the sourdough starter to the dry ingredients. Using a spoon, mix all the ingredients together until a dough starts to form.
4. Transfer the dough onto a gluten-free floured surface and knead it for about 10 minutes until it becomes elastic and non-sticky.
5. Once kneaded, shape the dough into a smooth ball and place it in a greased bowl. Cover the bowl with a clean towel and let it proof for about 2 hours in a warm place until it doubles in size.
6. Preheat the oven to 450 F and lightly brush a loaf pan with some olive oil.
7. Once the dough has risen, punch it down to release the air and shape it into a loaf. Place this loaf into the prepared pan.
8. Let the loaf proof for another 20 minutes in the pan before baking.
9. Place the pan in the preheated oven and bake for about 40 minutes or until the loaf sounds hollow when tapped on the bottom.
10. Once baked, remove the bread from the oven and let it cool on a wire rack.
11. Serve your herbs de Provence sourdough loaf with some butter or olive oil for a perfect gluten-free treat!

LEMON & DILL SOURDOUGH LOAF

Preparation Time: 1 hour and 20 minutes
Cooking Time: 40 minutes

INGREDIENTS:
- 3 1/2 cups of gluten-free bread mix
- 1 1/2 tsp of salt
- 1 tsp of gluten-free active dry yeast
- 2 tbsp of olive oil
- 1 cup of gluten-free sourdough starter
- 1 cup of warm water (+/- depending on the gluten-free mix)
- Zest of two medium-sized lemons
- 1/4 cup of fresh dill, finely chopped
- 2 tbsp of lemon juice
- Additional gluten-free flour for dusting

INSTRUCTIONS:
1. In a large bowl, combine the gluten-free bread mix, salt, and yeast together.
2. In a separate bowl, mix the gluten-free sourdough starter with warm water.
3. Gradually add the wet mixture into the dry ingredients, stirring continuously. The dough should form a ball and have some elasticity, while slightly sticking to the bottom of the bowl.
4. Mix in the olive oil, lemon zest, dill, and lemon juice until evenly distributed.
5. Lightly dust the working surface with gluten-free flour and transfer the dough onto it. Knead for around 5 minutes until the dough is smooth.
6. Place the dough back into the bowl, cover with a damp cloth and let it rise for about 1 hour.
7. Preheat the oven to 450F degrees. Place the dough in a greased bread pan.
8. Let it rise for another 20 minutes.
9. Bake for 40 minutes in the preheated oven until the crust is golden brown and the loaf sounds hollow when tapped beneath.
10. Let the loaf cool completely before slicing and serving.
11. Enjoy your homemade gluten-free lemon & dill sourdough loaf!

LEMON & ROSEMARY SOURDOUGH BAGUETTE

Preparation Time: 180 minutes
Cooking Time: 25 minutes

INGREDIENTS:

- 3 1/2 cups gluten-free bread flour
- 1 tsp salt
- 1 1/2 cups sourdough starter
- Zest of 1 lemon
- 2 sprigs fresh rosemary (chopped)
- 1 1/4 cups water
- 1 tsp sugar
- 1 tbsp olive oil
- 1 egg white (for brushing on top)

INSTRUCTIONS:

1. In a large bowl, combine the gluten-free bread flour, salt, sugar, and lemon zest.
2. Mix in the sourdough starter, chopped rosemary, and water. Beat until the dough forms into a ball.
3. Knead the dough on a lightly floured surface until smooth, approximately 7-10 minutes.
4. Place the dough in a greased bowl and coat the top with olive oil. Cover and let rise in a warm place for about 2 hours, until it doubles in size.
5. Preheat your oven to 450 degrees F and line a baking sheet with parchment paper.
6. Once the dough has risen, punch it down gently and divide it into two parts. Roll each part into a log shape, creating two baguettes.
7. Place the baguettes on the prepared baking sheet, cover, and let them rest for about 30 minutes.
8. Before popping them in the oven, make diagonal slashes on the baguettes using a sharp knife, then brush them with the egg white.
9. Bake for 20-25 minutes, until golden brown.
10. Let the baguettes cool before slicing and serving.

OLIVE & HERB SOURDOUGH BAGUETTE

Preparation Time: 180 minutes
Cooking Time: 25 minutes

INGREDIENTS:

- 3 1/2 cups of gluten-free all-purpose flour
- 1 cup of gluten-free sourdough starter
- 2 teaspoons of xanthan gum
- 1 1/2 teaspoons of salt
- 1 cup of warm water

- 11/2 tablespoons of honey
- 2 tablespoons of olive oil
- 1/4 cup of chopped fresh herbs (parsley, rosemary, and thyme)
- 1/2 cup of pitted and sliced black olives
- 1 teaspoon of apple cider vinegar
- Cornmeal for dusting
- Olive oil for brushing

INSTRUCTIONS:
1. In a large bowl, combine the gluten-free flour, sourdough starter, xanthan gum, and salt.
2. In a separate bowl, mix the warm water and honey until the honey is completely dissolved. Add the olive oil into the mixture.
3. Gradually add the olive oil and water mixture into the flour mixture, stirring continuously until you've formed a thick, sticky dough.
4. Fold in the chopped herbs and sliced olives until evenly distributed throughout the dough.
5. Add in the apple cider vinegar, folding it into the dough.
6. Cover the dough and let it rise for about 2-3 hours, or until it has roughly doubled in size.
7. Preheat your oven to 450°F (230°C) and lightly dust your baking tray with cornmeal.
8. Once the dough has risen, divide it into two equal parts, and shape each one into a long, thin baguette shape.
9. Place the baguettes onto the prepared baking tray, make diagonal slashes across the top of each baguette using a sharp knife, and brush them lightly with olive oil.
10. Bake in the preheated oven for 25-30 minutes or until the baguettes are golden brown and sound hollow when tapped on the bottom.
11. Remove from oven and let cool before slicing to serve.

ONION & CHIVE SOURDOUGH BAGUETTE

Preparation Time: 75 minutes
Cooking Time: 30 minutes

INGREDIENTS:
- 1 cup sourdough starter
- 1 cup warm water
- 2 1/2 cups gluten-free flour blend
- 2 teaspoons xanthan gum
- 1 1/2 teaspoons salt

- 2 tablespoons olive oil
- 1 tablespoon honey
- 1 packet (2 1/4 teaspoons) active dry yeast
- 2 tablespoons dried onion flakes
- 1/4 cup chopped fresh chives
- 1 egg (for egg wash)
- Coarse sea salt (for topping)

INSTRUCTIONS:
1. In a large bowl, combine warm water and yeast. Allow it to sit for 5 minutes until it bubbles.
2. Mix in sourdough starter, gluten-free flour blend, xanthan gum, salt, olive oil, honey, dried onion flakes, and chopped chives.
3. Beat the dough with an electric mixer for about 7 minutes—until smooth and elastic.
4. Cover the dough and let it proof in a warm, draft-free area for about one hour until it doubles in size.
5. Preheat your oven to 450°F (230°C). Position a baking stone in the middle of the oven and a baking tray filled with water at the bottom for steam.
6. Shape your dough into a baguette form on a piece of parchment paper.
7. Carefully transfer the shaped dough with the parchment paper onto the pre-heated baking stone.
8. Immediately reduce the oven temperature to 425°F (220°C).
9. Bake for 30 minutes until the baguette is golden brown.
10. Cool completely on a wire rack before slicing and serving.

NO-YEAST PASTRIES

APPLE TURNOVERS

Preparation time: 80 minutes
Cooking time: 15 minutes

INGREDIENTS:
For the gluten-free pastry:
- 1 cup gluten-free flour
- 1/4 teaspoon xanthan gum (if your gluten-free flour doesn't contain it)
- 3 tablespoons granulated sugar
- 1/2 cup (1 stick) unsalted butter, cold and cut into small pieces
- 1 large egg

For the apple filling:
- 3 Gala apples, peeled and finely chopped
- 2 tablespoons unsalted butter
- 1/4 cup granulated sugar
- 1/4 cup brown sugar
- 2 teaspoons cinnamon
- 1/4 teaspoon nutmeg

For the glaze:
- 1/2 cup powdered sugar
- 1-2 tablespoons milk

INSTRUCTIONS:
1. In a bowl, combine the gluten-free flour, xanthan gum (if using), sugar, and butter. Blend together with a pastry cutter or fingers until the mixture resembles coarse crumbs.
2. Add the egg to the flour mixture and stir just until the dough comes together. Form the dough into a disk, wrap in plastic wrap, and refrigerate for at least 1 hour.
3. Preheat the oven to 30 degrees F (10 degrees C). Line a baking sheet with parchment paper.
4. In a large skillet over medium heat, melt the butter. Add the chopped apples, granulated sugar, brown sugar, cinnamon, and nutmeg. Cook until the apples are softened, and the liquid has evaporated, about 10-minutes.
5. Remove the dough from the fridge and roll out on a lightly floured surface to about 1/8-inch thickness. Using a round cookie cutter (or the rim of a glass), cut out circles from the dough.

6. Place a small spoonful of the apple mixture onto the center of each dough circle. Fold the dough over the filling and press the edges together with a fork to seal.
7. Place the turnovers onto the prepared baking sheet, and bake in the preheated oven for about 15 minutes, or until golden brown.
8. While the turnovers are baking, mix together the powdered sugar and milk to create a glaze. Drizzle the glaze over the still-warm turnovers before serving.

BANANA CREAM TARTS

Preparation time: 140 minutes
Cooking time: 15 minutes

INGREDIENTS:
For the crust:
- 2 cups gluten-free graham cracker crumbs
- 1/2 cup unsalted butter, melted
- 1/4 cup granulated sugar

For the banana cream filling:
- 3 ripe bananas
- 2 cups whole milk
- 1/2 cup granulated sugar
- 1/4 cup cornstarch
- 4 large egg yolks
- 1 teaspoon pure vanilla extract
- Pinch of salt

For the whipped cream:
- 1 cup heavy cream
- 2 tablespoons powdered sugar
- 1 teaspoon pure vanilla extract

INSTRUCTIONS:
1. Preheat your oven to 350°F (180°C) and lightly grease a 12-cup muffin tin.
2. Combine the graham cracker crumbs, melted butter and sugar in a bowl and mix until all crumbs are moistened. Divide this mixture evenly among the muffin cups, pressing it into the bottom and up the sides.
3. Bake the crusts for about 15 minutes, until they are set and slightly golden. Let them cool completely in the muffin tin.

4. To make the banana cream filling, puree the bananas in a blender or food processor until smooth. Set aside.
5. In a medium saucepan, combine the milk, sugar, cornstarch, egg yolks, vanilla extract, and salt. Cook over medium heat, stirring constantly, until the mixture thickens and bubbles.
6. Stir in the pureed bananas until well mixed. Let the banana cream mixture cool slightly, then divide it evenly among the cooled crusts.
7. Place the tarts in the refrigerator to chill for at least 2 hours, or until the banana cream is set.
8. Just before serving, make the whipped cream. Whip the heavy cream, powdered sugar, and vanilla extract in a large bowl until soft peaks form.
9. Top each tart with a dollop of whipped cream.

CINNAMON ROLLS

Preparation Time: 30 minutes
Cooking Time: 35 minutes

INGREDIENTS:
For the dough:
- 2 3/4 cups gluten-free flour blend
- 1/4 cup granulated sugar
- 1 1/4 teaspoons baking powder
- 1/2 teaspoon baking soda
- 1/2 teaspoon salt
- 1 package (or 2 1/4 teaspoons) active dry yeast
- 1 cup warm milk
- 1/4 cup unsalted butter, melted
- 1 large egg

For the filling:
- 1 cup packed light brown sugar
- 2 tablespoons ground cinnamon
- 1/4 cup melted butter

For the icing:
- 1/2 cup powdered sugar
- 3-4 tablespoons milk
- 1/2 teaspoon vanilla extract

INSTRUCTIONS:
1. In a large bowl, wet blend together milk, butter, yeast, and egg. In a separate bowl, dry blend together the gluten-free flour blend, sugar, baking powder, baking soda, and salt.
2. Gradually add the dry mixture into the wet mixture, stirring until thoroughly combined. Let the dough rest for a few minutes.
3. Create the filling by mixing the brown sugar and cinnamon in a small bowl. Set aside.
4. Turn your dough onto a well-floured surface. Using a rolling pin, roll out your dough into a rough rectangle, about 1/2 inch in thickness
5. Brush your rolled dough with the melted butter. Sprinkle the cinnamon sugar mixture evenly across the dough.
6. Carefully roll your dough up into a log, starting from one of the long edges.
7. Slice the dough into rounds, each about 1 inch thick. This should make about 12 rolls.
8. Place your rolls on a baking sheet lined with parchment paper or in a greased baking dish.
9. Bake at 375 degrees Fahrenheit for 25-30 minutes or until lightly golden brown.
10. While the rolls are cooling, mix the powdered sugar, milk, and vanilla extract in a bowl until smooth. Adjust according to your preferred thickness.
11. Drizzle icing over the top of cooled cinnamon rolls, serve and enjoy!

CROISSANTS

Preparation Time: 3 hours
Cooking Time: 20 minutes

INGREDIENTS:
- 2 cups of gluten-free all-purpose flour
- 1/4 cup of sugar
- 1 tablespoon of baking powder
- 1 teaspoon of xanthan gum (omit if your flour blend contains it)
- 1/2 teaspoon of salt
- 1/4 cup of cold unsalted butter, cut into small pieces
- 2 large eggs
- 1/2 cup of cold milk
- 1 teaspoon of apple cider vinegar
- 1/2 cup of gluten-free flour for dusting
- 1/2 cup of melted butter for brushing
- 1/2 cup of powdered sugar for dusting

INSTRUCTIONS:
1. In a large bowl, mix the gluten-free all-purpose flour, sugar, baking powder, xanthan gum (if using), and salt.
2. Add the cold butter pieces to the flour mixture and cut in using a pastry cutter or your fingers. The mixture should look like coarse crumbs.
3. In a separate bowl, whisk together the eggs, cold milk, and apple cider vinegar until well combined.
4. Gradually add the wet ingredients to the flour mixture, stirring until the dough comes together.
5. Turn the dough onto a heavily floured surface. Knead the dough a few times until it is no longer sticky.
6. Roll the dough into a large rectangle about 1/2-inch thick.
7. Brush the dough with some of the melted butter.
8. Carefully roll the dough into a log, starting from the longest edge. Cut the log into 8 even pieces.
9. Place the pieces on a baking sheet lined with parchment paper, making sure they are at least 2 inches apart.
10. Allow the croissants to rest in a warm place for about 1 to 2 hours, or until they have doubled in size.
11. Preheat your oven to 375°F (190°C).
12. Bake the croissants for 15-20 minutes, or until they are golden brown.
13. Let the croissants cool slightly then dust with powdered sugar before serving.
14. Enjoy your homemade gluten-free croissants, perfect for breakfast, brunch, or any time of day!

DANISH PASTRY WITH CREAM CHEESE FILLING

Preparation Time: 45 minutes
Cooking Time: 25 minutes

INGREDIENTS:
For the Danish pastry:
- 2 cups gluten-free flour blend
- 1 tablespoon xanthan gum (skip if your gluten-free flour blend includes this)
- 2 teaspoons gluten-free baking powder
- 1/2 cup granulated sugar
- 1/2 teaspoon salt
- 1 cup unsalted butter, cold and cut into small pieces
- 2 large eggs

- 1/4 cup milk
- 1 teaspoon gluten-free vanilla extract

For the cream cheese filling:
- 8 ounces cream cheese, softened
- 1/4 cup granulated sugar
- 1 large egg yolk
- 1 teaspoon gluten-free vanilla extract
- 1 tablespoon gluten-free flour blend

INSTRUCTIONS:
1. Preheat your oven to 375 degrees Fahrenheit and line a baking sheet with parchment paper.
2. In a large bowl, combine the gluten-free flour blend, xanthan gum (if using), baking powder, sugar, and salt.
3. Add the cold, chopped butter to the flour mixture. Use your fingers to rub the butter into the flour until the mixture looks like coarse breadcrumbs.
4. In another bowl, whisk together the eggs, milk, and vanilla extract. Pour this wet mixture into the flour mixture and stir until a dough forms.
5. Knead the dough a few times on a lightly gluten-free floured surface until it comes together. Roll out the dough until it's about 1/2 inch thick.
6. Cut the dough into squares or circles (as desired), then transfer them to the parchment-lined baking sheet.
7. For the filling, beat together the cream cheese, sugar, egg yolk, vanilla extract, and gluten-free flour in a separate bowl until smooth and creamy.
8. Spoon a dollop of the cream cheese filling onto the center of each pastry.
9. Fold the edges of the pastries over the filling and gently pinch to seal.
10. Bake the pastries in the preheated oven for about 25 minutes, or until golden brown.
11. Enjoy these delectable gluten-free Danishes with a cup of coffee in the morning or as a special dessert. They are perfect for anyone with gluten restrictions or those who simply prefer a gluten-free diet.

ÉCLAIRS

Preparation Time: 45 minutes
Cooking Time: 20 minutes

INGREDIENTS:
For the eclairs:
- 1 cup of water

- 1/2 cup (1 stick) unsalted butter
- 1/2 teaspoon salt
- 1 1/4 cups gluten-free flour
- 4 large eggs

For the filling:
- 1 1/2 cups whole milk
- 1 teaspoon pure vanilla extract
- 3 large egg yolks
- 1/4 cup granulated sugar
- 2 tablespoons cornstarch
- 2 tablespoons unsalted butter

For the chocolate glaze:
- 3 ounces semi-sweet chocolate, finely chopped
- 1/2 cup heavy cream
- 1 tablespoon corn syrup

INSTRUCTIONS:
1. Preheat your oven to 425°F (220°C). Line a baking sheet with parchment paper.
2. In a medium saucepan, heat water, butter, and salt over medium heat until butter is melted, and it begins to boil.
3. Reduce heat to low, add gluten-free flour all at once, stirring vigorously with a wooden spoon. Continue to stir until mixture forms a ball and leaves a film on the bottom of the pan, about 1 minute
4. Remove from heat and let cool for 5 minutes.
5. Beat in the eggs, one at a time, ensuring each egg is fully incorporated before adding the next.
6. Drop dough by rounded tablespoon-fulls onto the prepared baking sheet, spacing about 2 inches apart.
7. Bake for 20 minutes in the preheated oven, until golden brown. Remove from the oven and let cool on the pan.
8. In a medium saucepan, heat the milk over medium-high heat until it just starts to bubble around the edges.
9. In a separate bowl, whisk together egg yolks, sugar, and cornstarch until smooth.
10. While whisking constantly, slowly pour the hot milk into the egg mixture.
11. Return the mixture to the pot and cook over medium heat, whisking constantly until it thickens.

12. Remove from heat and stir in butter and vanilla extract. Pour into a bowl and cover with plastic wrap, pressing it directly onto the surface of the pastry cream to prevent a skin from forming. Refrigerate until chilled, about 2 hours.
13. Place the chopped chocolate in a bowl. In a small saucepan, heat the cream and corn syrup until just boiling. Pour the mixture over the chocolate and let stand for 3-5 minutes.
14. Stir until smooth. Let cool until slightly thickened.
15. Cut a small hole in the bottom of each cooled éclair shell.
16. Fill each shell with the chilled pastry cream. Dip the tops of the filled éclairs into the chocolate glaze.
17. Allow the éclairs to sit for a few minutes for the glaze to set. Serve and enjoy!

LEMON BARS

Preparation Time: 20 minutes
Cooking Time: 40 minutes

INGREDIENTS:
Crust ingredients:
- 1 cup of gluten-free flour
- 1/4 cup of granulated sugar
- 1/2 cup of unsalted butter (cold and cut into small pieces)

Filling ingredients:
- 1 cup of granulated sugar
- 2 large eggs
- 1/2 cup of fresh lemon juice (about 2 lemons)
- 2 tablespoons of gluten-free flour
- Zest of 1 lemon
- Confectioners' sugar for dusting

INSTRUCTIONS:
1. Preheat your oven to 350°F (180°C) and line an 8x8 inch baking pan with parchment paper.
2. Start by making the crust. In a medium bowl, combine gluten-free flour, sugar, and cold butter. Use a fork or pastry blender to cut the butter into the flour until the mixture resembles fine breadcrumbs.
3. Press the crust mixture evenly into the bottom of the parchment lined pan. Bake in the preheated oven for about 15-20 minutes, or until lightly golden.

4. While the crust is baking, prepare the lemon filling. In a separate bowl, combine sugar, eggs, fresh lemon juice, gluten-free flour, and lemon zest. Whisk until well mixed.
5. Once the crust is ready, reduce the oven temperature to 325°F (165°C). Pour the lemon filling over the hot crust.
6. Return the pan to the oven and bake for an additional 20 minutes, or until the filling is set and doesn't jiggle when the pan is gently shaken.
7. Remove from the oven and let it cool completely at room temperature. Once cool, place in the refrigerator for at least 2 hours to allow the lemon bars to fully set.
8. Before serving, dust the top of the lemon bars with confectioners' sugar. Cut them into squares and serve.

MIXED BERRY TARTS

Preparation Time: 30 minutes
Cooking Time: 15 minutes

INGREDIENTS:
For the crust:
- 2 cups gluten-free flour
- 1/2 cup unsalted butter, chilled and diced
- 1/4 cup granulated sugar
- 1/4 teaspoon salt
- 1 large egg
- 2-4 tablespoons cold water

For the filling:
- 4 cups mixed berries (blueberries, raspberries, strawberries, and blackberries)
- 1/2 cup granulated sugar
- 1 tablespoon lemon juice
- 1 tablespoon cornstarch
- 1 tablespoon cold water

INSTRUCTIONS:
1. Start by preheating your oven to 375°F (190°C).
2. In a large bowl, combine gluten-free flour, sugar, salt, and chilled butter. Using your fingers, work the butter into the flour until the mixture resembles coarse meal.
3. Add in the egg, mix until just combined. Gradually drizzle in the cold water, starting with 2 tablespoons and add more if needed, until a dough forms.

4. Turn out onto a lightly floured surface and knead gently until smooth. Divide the dough into six portions and press each into the bottom and up the sides of a 4-inch tart pan.

5. Prick the bottom of crust all over with a fork, then bake until lightly golden, about 12 minutes.

6. While the crusts are baking, make your berry mixture. In a large saucepan over medium heat, combine the mixed berries, sugar, and lemon juice. Bring to a simmer, stirring occasionally until the sugar has dissolved.

7. In a small bowl, mix together the cornstarch and cold water to create a slurry, then stir this into the berry mixture. Continue to cook, stirring frequently, until the mixture has thickened, about 5-7 minutes.

8. Remove the baked tart shells from the oven and divide the berry filling equally among them.

9. Return the tarts to the oven and bake 5-7 minutes longer, or until the filling is set.

10. Allow the tarts to cool completely before serving.

PEACH GALETTE

Preparation Time: 15 minutes
Cooking Time: 10 minutes

INGREDIENTS:
For the gluten-free galette dough:
- 1 cup of gluten-free baking flour
- 1 tablespoon of granulated sugar
- 1/4 teaspoon of salt
- 6 tablespoons of cold unsalted butter, cut into pieces
- 4 to 6 tablespoons of ice water

Filling:
- 4-5 ripe peaches, pitted and thinly sliced
- 1/4 cup of granulated sugar
- 1 tablespoon of gluten-free flour
- 1/4 teaspoon of ground cinnamon
- 1 tablespoon of lemon juice

For Finishing:
- 1 egg beaten, for egg wash
- 2 tablespoons of granulated sugar, for sprinkling
- 1/4 teaspoon of ground cinnamon, for sprinkling

INSTRUCTIONS:
1. Start with the gluten-free galette dough. In a bowl, combine flour, sugar, and salt.
2. Add the cold butter pieces. Using your fingers, quickly break the butter into the flour until it resembles coarse crumbs.
3. Gradually add the ice water and mix it into the dough until it holds together when squeezed. Add more water, 1 tablespoon at a time, if necessary.
4. Flatten the dough into a disk, wrap it in plastic, and refrigerate for at least 1 hour.
5. Preheat your oven to 375°F (190°C) and line a baking sheet with parchment paper.
6. Meanwhile, prepare the filling. Combine sliced peaches, sugar, flour, cinnamon, and lemon juice in a large bowl. Gently toss together until the peaches are well-coated.
7. Roll out the chilled dough in a circle on a piece of lightly floured parchment paper. It doesn't need to be perfect, as the galette is meant to be rustic.
8. Arrange the peach slices on top of the dough, leaving a 2-inch border around the edge. Fold the edges of the dough over the peaches, pleating it as you go.
9. Brush the dough with the beaten egg. Sprinkle sugar and cinnamon over the entire galette.
10. Bake for approximately 10 minutes, or until the crust is golden and the peach filling is bubbling. Allow the galette to cool slightly before serving.

PINEAPPLE UPSIDE-DOWN MINI CAKES

Preparation Time: 25 minutes
Cooking Time: 30 minutes

INGREDIENTS:
For the topping:
- 8 slices of canned pineapple, drained
- 8 maraschino cherries
- 1/2 cup packed light brown sugar
- 4 tablespoons unsalted butter, melted

For the cakes:
- 1 3/4 cups gluten-free baking flour
- 1 1/2 teaspoons baking powder
- 1/2 teaspoon baking soda
- 1/2 teaspoon salt
- 1/2 cup unsalted butter, softened
- 3/4 cup granulated sugar
- 2 large eggs

- 1 teaspoon pure vanilla extract
- 3/4 cup buttermilk

INSTRUCTIONS:
1. Preheat your oven to 350°F (180°C). Liberally grease a non-stick muffin pan.
2. Prepare the topping by combining the melted butter and brown sugar in a small bowl. Divide this mixture evenly among the muffin cups.
3. Place a pineapple slice inside each muffin cup, fitting it snugly at the base. Place a cherry in the center of each pineapple slice.
4. In a large bowl, whisk together the gluten-free flour, baking powder, baking soda, and salt.
5. In a separate bowl, beat the softened butter and granulated sugar until the mixture is fluffy. Add the eggs, one at a time, beating well after each addition. Stir in the vanilla extract.
6. Gradually add the flour mixture to the wet ingredients, alternating with the buttermilk, beginning and ending with the flour mixture. Mix until just combined.
7. Spoon the batter into the prepared muffin cups, filling each three-quarters full.
8. Bake for 25 minutes, or until a toothpick inserted into the center of a cake comes out clean.
9. Allow the cakes to cool in the pan on a wire rack for 5 minutes. Then invert the pan onto the rack, gently removing the cakes.
10. Serve the mini cakes warm or at room temperature, pineapple-side up.

PUFF PASTRY TARTS

Preparation Time: 60 minutes
Cooking Time: 25 minutes

INGREDIENTS:
For the puff pastry:
- 1 cup of Bob's Red Mill Gluten-Free 1 to 1 Baking Flour
- Pinch of salt
- 1/2 cup of unsalted butter, cold and cubed
- 1/3 cup of ice cold water

For the filling:
- 4 medium apples, peeled and thinly sliced
- 1/4 cup of granulated sugar
- 2 tablespoons of lemon juice
- 1/2 teaspoon of cinnamon

For the glaze:
- 1/4 cup of apricot jam
- 1 tablespoon of water

INSTRUCTIONS:
1. Start by making the pastry. In a large bowl, mix the gluten-free flour and salt together. Add the cold, cubed butter and use your hands to rub it into the flour until it resembles breadcrumbs.
2. Gradually add the ice cold water, stirring until the dough comes together.
3. Shape the dough into a rectangle, then wrap in clingfilm and chill for 30 minutes in the fridge.
4. After 30 minutes, roll the dough into a 15x10 inch rectangle, then fold into thirds like a letter. Rotate the dough 90 degrees and repeat this process twice.
5. Wrap the dough again and chill for another 30 minutes.
6. Preheat your oven to 400°F (200°C) and line a baking sheet with parchment paper.
7. While the dough chills, prepare your filling. Combine the sliced apples, sugar, lemon juice, and cinnamon in a bowl, then set aside.
8. Once the dough has chilled, roll it once more into a 15x10 inch rectangle, then cut into six smaller rectangles.
9. Place a handful of filling onto one half of each rectangle, fold the other half over, and crimp the edges to seal.
10. Transfer the tarts to the prepared baking sheet, then bake for 20-25 minutes, or until golden brown.
11. Meanwhile, heat the apricot jam and water in a pan until it forms a glaze. Once the pastries are done, brush them with this glaze for a shiny finish.
12. Allow the tarts to cool slightly before serving.

SCONES WITH JAM

Preparation Time: 20 minutes
Cooking Time: 15 minutes

INGREDIENTS:
- 2 cups of all-purpose gluten-free flour
- 1/3 cup of granulated sugar
- 1 tablespoon of gluten-free baking powder
- 1/2 teaspoon of xanthan gum (if your flour blend doesn't include it)
- 1/2 teaspoon of salt
- 1/2 cup (1 stick) of cold unsalted butter, cut into small pieces

- 2/3 cup of whole milk
- 1 large egg
- 1 teaspoon of pure vanilla extract
- Your favorite gluten-free jam for serving

INSTRUCTIONS:
1. Preheat your oven to 425°F (220°C) and line a baking sheet with parchment paper.
2. In a large bowl, combine the gluten-free flour, sugar, baking powder, xanthan gum (if using), and salt.
3. Add the cold butter to the flour mixture. Using a pastry cutter or your fingers, cut the butter into the flour until it resembles coarse crumbs.
4. In a separate bowl, whisk together the milk, egg, and vanilla extract. Gradually add this to the flour mixture, stirring until just combined. Do not overmix.
5. Using a spoon or your hands, drop the dough onto the prepared baking sheet, shaping it into rounds. Leave at least 1 1/2 inches between each scone.
6. Bake for about 15 minutes, or until the scones are golden.
7. Remove the scones from the oven and let them cool on the baking sheet for a few minutes, then transfer them to a wire rack to cool further.
8. Once the scones are cooled, cut them in half and spread with your favorite gluten-free jam. Enjoy your homemade gluten-free scones with jam!

MUFFINS

APPLE CINNAMON MUFFINS

Preparation Time: 20 minutes
Cooking Time: 25 minutes

INGREDIENTS:
- 2 cups gluten-free flour mix
- 1 tablespoon baking powder
- 1/2 teaspoon salt
- 2 teaspoons ground cinnamon
- 1/2 cup unsalted butter, room temperature
- 1 cup granulated sugar
- 2 large eggs
- 1 teaspoon pure vanilla extract
- 3/4 cup buttermilk
- 2 medium apples, peeled, cored, and diced

For topping:
- 2 tablespoons granulated sugar
- 1 teaspoon ground cinnamon

INSTRUCTIONS:
1. Preheat your oven to 375°F (190°C) and line a muffin pan with paper liners or lightly grease with cooking spray.
2. In a medium-sized bowl, mix gluten-free flour, baking powder, salt, and cinnamon. Set aside.
3. In a large bowl, cream together the butter and sugar until it's light and fluffy. This should take about 2 minutes.
4. Beat in the eggs, one at a time, then stir in the vanilla extract.
5. Gradually add the flour mixture to the butter mixture, alternating with buttermilk. Begin and end with the flour mixture. Stir just until combined.
6. Fold in the diced apples.
7. Scoop the batter into the prepared muffin pan, filling each cup about 2/3 full.
8. In a small bowl, mix the sugar and cinnamon for the topping. Sprinkle this mixture evenly over the tops of the muffins.
9. Bake in the preheated oven for about 25 minutes, or until a toothpick inserted into the center of a muffin comes out clean.
10. Allow the muffins to cool in the pan for 5 minutes before transferring them to a wire rack to finish cooling.

BANANA BREAD MUFFINS

Preparation Time: 15 minutes
Cooking Time: 25 minutes

INGREDIENTS:
- 1 1/2 cups of gluten-free baking flour
- 1 1/2 teaspoons of baking powder
- 1/2 teaspoon of baking soda
- 1/4 teaspoon of salt
- 1 teaspoon of cinnamon
- 3 ripe bananas
- 1/3 cup of melted unsalted butter
- 3/4 cup of granulated sugar
- 1 large egg
- 1 teaspoon of pure vanilla extract
- 1/2 cup of chopped walnuts or pecans

INSTRUCTIONS:
1. Preheat your oven to 350°F (175°C) and line a muffin tin with paper liners.
2. In a mixing bowl, whisk together the gluten-free baking flour, baking powder, baking soda, salt, and cinnamon.
3. In a separate large bowl, mash the ripe bananas. Then add the melted butter, granulated sugar, egg, and vanilla extract. Stir until well combined.
4. Gradually add the dry ingredient mixture to the banana mixture, stirring until just combined.
5. Fold in the chopped walnuts or pecans.
6. Divide the batter evenly among the muffin cups, filling each about 3/4 full.
7. Bake for 25 minutes, or until a toothpick inserted into the center of a muffin comes out clean.
8. Allow the muffins to cool in the pan for 10 minutes, then transfer them to a wire rack to cool completely.

BANANA NUT MUFFINS

Preparation Time: 15 minutes
Cooking Time: 25 minutes

INGREDIENTS:
- 2 ripe bananas, peeled
- 2 large eggs

- 1 teaspoon pure vanilla extract
- 1/2 cup almond butter
- 1/4 cup unsalted butter, melted
- 2 cups almond flour
- 1/2 cup sugar
- 1/4 cup brown sugar
- 1 teaspoon baking soda
- 1/2 teaspoon salt
- 1 cup walnuts, chopped
- 1/2 cup raisins or chocolate chips (optional)

INSTRUCTIONS:
1. Preheat your oven to 350°F (175°C) and line a muffin tin with paper liners.
2. In a large bowl, mash the bananas until smooth. Stir in the eggs, vanilla extract, almond butter, and melted butter until well combined.
3. In another bowl, combine the almond flour, sugar, brown sugar, baking soda, and salt. Mix well to combine.
4. Gradually add the dry ingredients to the banana mixture, mixing just until combined. Be careful not to overmix.
5. Fold in the chopped walnuts and optional raisins or chocolate chips.
6. Divide the batter evenly among the prepared muffin cups, filling each to about 3/4 full.
7. Bake in the preheated oven for 20-25 minutes, or until the muffins are golden brown and a toothpick inserted in the center comes out clean.
8. Remove the muffins from the oven and allow them to cool in the pan for 5 minutes.
9. After 5 minutes, transfer the muffins to a wire rack to cool completely.

BLACKBERRY LEMON MUFFINS

Preparation Time: 15 minutes
Cooking Time: 25 minutes

INGREDIENTS:
- 2 cups of gluten-free all-purpose flour
- 2 teaspoons of baking powder
- 1/2 teaspoon of salt
- 1/2 cup of unsalted butter, room temperature
- 1 cup of granulated sugar
- 2 large eggs

- 1/2 teaspoon of pure vanilla extract
- 2 tablespoons of lemon zest (from about 2 lemons)
- 1/4 cup of freshly squeezed lemon juice
- 1/2 cup of whole milk
- 1 1/2 cups of fresh blackberries

INSTRUCTIONS:
1. Preheat oven to 375°F (190°C) and prepare a muffin pan by either greasing it or using paper liners.
2. In a large bowl, whisk together the gluten-free flour, baking powder, and salt.
3. In another bowl, beat the butter and sugar together with an electric mixer until smooth and creamy. Add the eggs, one at a time, beating well after each addition.
4. Stir in the vanilla extract, lemon zest, and lemon juice.
5. Gradually add the flour mixture in three parts, alternating with the milk, beginning and ending with the flour. Stir just until the batter is smooth.
6. Gently fold in the blackberries.
7. Spoon the batter into the prepared muffin tins, filling each cup about 2/3 full.
8. Bake for 25 minutes, or until a toothpick inserted into the center of a muffin comes out clean.
9. Allow the muffins to cool in the pan for 5 minutes, then transfer to a wire rack to cool completely.

BLUEBERRY MUFFINS

Preparation Time: 15 minutes
Cooking Time: 20 minutes

INGREDIENTS:
- 2 cups gluten-free all-purpose flour
- 2 teaspoons baking powder
- 1/2 teaspoon baking soda
- 1/4 teaspoon salt
- 3/4 cup granulated sugar
- 1 cup unsweetened almond milk
- 1/3 cup melted coconut oil
- 2 large eggs
- 1 teaspoon pure vanilla extract
- 1 1/2 cups fresh or frozen blueberries
- Zest from 1 lemon

INSTRUCTIONS:
1. Preheat your oven to 375°F (190°C). Grease a standard-size muffin tin or line with paper liners.
2. In a large bowl, whisk together the gluten-free flour, baking powder, baking soda, salt, and sugar.
3. In another bowl, combine the almond milk, melted coconut oil, eggs, and pure vanilla extract. Mix well.
4. Gradually add the wet ingredients to the dry ingredients, stirring until just combined.
5. Gently fold in the blueberries and lemon zest.
6. Spoon the batter into the prepared muffin tin, filling each cup about 2/3 full.
7. Bake for 20-22 minutes, or until the tops of the muffins are firm and a toothpick inserted into the center comes out clean.
8. Let the muffins cool in the tin for 5 minutes, then remove and let them cool on a wire rack.
9. Enjoy your gluten-free blueberry muffins warm or store them in an airtight container at room temperature for up to 3 days.

CARROT CAKE MUFFINS

Preparation Time: 20 minutes
Cooking Time: 25 minutes

INGREDIENTS:
- 1 cup of gluten-free all-purpose flour
- 1/2 cup of almond flour
- 1 teaspoon of baking soda
- 1/4 teaspoon of fine sea salt
- 1 1/2 teaspoons of ground cinnamon
- 1/4 teaspoon of ground nutmeg
- 3/4 cup of granulated sugar
- 2 large eggs
- 1/2 cup of vegetable oil
- 1 teaspoon of pure vanilla extract
- 1 1/2 cups of finely grated carrots
- 1/2 cup of crushed pineapple, drained
- 1/2 cup of unsweetened shredded coconut
- 1/2 cup of raisins

INSTRUCTIONS:

1. Preheat your oven to 350°F (175°C) and place paper liners into a muffin pan.
2. In a medium-sized bowl, combine the gluten-free all-purpose flour, almond flour, baking soda, sea salt, cinnamon, and nutmeg. Stir until these dry ingredients are well mixed.
3. In a larger bowl, whisk together the sugar, eggs, vegetable oil, and vanilla extract.
4. Gradually add the dry ingredient mix into the larger bowl with the wet ingredients. Stir until the batter is smooth and consistent.
5. Fold in the grated carrots, crushed pineapple, shredded coconut, and raisins into the batter, making sure they are evenly distributed.
6. Spoon the batter into the muffin liners, filling them about 3/4 of the way full.
7. Bake in your preheated oven for about 25 minutes. Check for doneness by inserting a toothpick into the center of a muffin. It should come out clean.
8. Remove the muffins from the oven and let them cool for about 5 minutes in the pan. After this, transfer the muffins to a wire rack so they can cool completely.
9. Enjoy your delicious, homemade gluten-free carrot cake muffins.

CHAI SPICE MUFFINS

Preparation Time: 20 minutes
Cooking Time: 20 minutes

INGREDIENTS:
- 2 cups gluten-free all-purpose flour
- 1 cup granulated sugar
- 1 tablespoon baking powder
- 1/2 teaspoon xanthan gum (if your gluten-free flour blend doesn't contain it)
- 1/2 teaspoon salt
- 1 tablespoon chai spice blend
- 1/2 cup unsalted butter, melted
- 2 large eggs
- 1 cup milk
- 1 teaspoon pure vanilla extract
- Chai sugar topping: 2 tablespoons granulated sugar mixed with 1/4 teaspoon chai spice blend

INSTRUCTIONS:
1. Preheat your oven to 375°F (190°C) and place your muffin liners in the muffin tin.
2. In a large bowl, combine your gluten-free flour, granulated sugar, baking powder, xanthan gum, salt, and chai spice blend. Stir until the ingredients are evenly distributed.

3. In another bowl, mix the melted butter, eggs, milk, and vanilla extract.
4. Slowly add your wet ingredients to the dry, stirring well after each addition. Continue until the batter is combined and smooth.
5. Using a spoon or ice cream scoop, distribute the batter evenly among the muffin cups, filling each one about 2/3 of the way full.
6. Sprinkle each muffin with the chai sugar topping.
7. Bake in the preheated oven for approximately 20 minutes, or until a toothpick inserted into the middle comes out clean.
8. Let the muffins cool in the pan for about 5 minutes, then remove them from the tin and place them on a wire rack to cool completely before serving.

CHOCOLATE CHIP MUFFINS

Preparation Time: 15 minutes
Cooking Time: 20 minutes

INGREDIENTS:
- 2 cups gluten-free all-purpose flour
- 1 cup granulated sugar
- 1 tablespoon baking powder
- 1/2 teaspoon salt
- 1/2 cup unsalted butter, melted
- 2 large eggs
- 1 cup whole milk
- 1 teaspoon pure vanilla extract
- 1 cup chocolate chips

INSTRUCTIONS:
1. Start by preheating your oven to 375°F (190°C). Then, line a muffin tin with paper liners.
2. In a large bowl, whisk together the gluten-free all-purpose flour, granulated sugar, baking powder, and salt.
3. In a separate, microwave-safe bowl, melt the unsalted butter. Allow it to cool slightly before proceeding.
4. In a smaller bowl, beat the two large eggs. Add these to the melted butter, mixing thoroughly.
5. Slowly pour the butter and egg mixture into the dry ingredients. Stir until everything is well combined.
6. Add in the whole milk and pure vanilla extract. Stir well to ensure that all the ingredients are evenly mixed.

7. Fold in the chocolate chips.
8. Using a scoop or a large spoon, fill each muffin cup about two-thirds full of the batter.
9. Bake in the preheated oven for about 20 minutes, or until a toothpick inserted into the center of a muffin comes out clean.
10. Allow the muffins to cool in the tin for 5 minutes before removing them and allowing them to cool completely on a wire rack.

DOUBLE CHOCOLATE MUFFINS

Preparation Time: 20 minutes
Cooking Time: 20 minutes

INGREDIENTS:
- 2 cups gluten-free flour
- 1/2 cup unsweetened cocoa powder
- 2 teaspoons gluten-free baking powder
- 1/2 teaspoon salt
- 1 cup granulated sugar
- 1/2 cup unsalted butter, melted
- 2 large eggs
- 1 cup whole milk
- 1 teaspoon pure vanilla extract
- 1 cup gluten-free chocolate chips

INSTRUCTIONS:
1. Preheat your oven to 375°F (190°C). Line a 12-cup muffin pan with paper liners or grease with non-stick spray.
2. In a large bowl, whisk together the gluten-free flour, cocoa powder, baking powder, and salt. Set aside.
3. In a medium bowl, mix the sugar and melted butter. Add the eggs, one at a time, beating well after each addition.
4. Stir in the milk and vanilla extract.
5. Add the wet ingredients to the dry ingredients and stir until just combined. Fold in the chocolate chips.
6. Divide the batter evenly among the muffin cups, filling each about 2/3 full.
7. Bake for 20 minutes, or until a toothpick inserted into the center of a muffin comes out clean.
8. Allow the muffins to cool in the pan for 5 minutes, then transfer them to a wire rack to cool completely.

LEMON POPPY SEED MUFFINS

Preparation Time: 15 minutes
Cooking Time: 20 minutes

INGREDIENTS:
- 2 cups of gluten-free all-purpose flour
- 1 tablespoon of baking powder
- 1/2 teaspoon of salt
- 3/4 cup of granulated sugar
- 2 tablespoons of poppy seeds
- Zest of 2 lemons
- 1/2 cup of unsalted butter, melted and cooled
- 2 large eggs
- 1 cup of milk (any kind, almond or oat milk for dairy-free)
- 1/2 teaspoon of gluten-free vanilla extract
- 1/4 cup of fresh lemon juice

INSTRUCTIONS:
1. Start by preheating your oven to 375 degrees F (190 degrees C) and line a 12-cup muffin pan with paper liners.
2. In a large bowl, mix the gluten-free all-purpose flour, baking powder, salt, granulated sugar, poppy seeds, and lemon zest. Make sure all the ingredients are fully combined.
3. In another bowl, whisk together the melted and cooled butter, eggs, milk, vanilla extract, and fresh lemon juice.
4. Create a well in the center of the dry ingredients, then pour the wet mixture into the well. Stir until the wet and dry ingredients are just combined. Do not overmix as it might make the muffins tough.
5. Evenly distribute the muffin batter among the lined muffin cups. They should be filled to about 2/3 full.
6. Bake in the preheated oven for 20 minutes or until a toothpick inserted into the center comes out clean.
7. Remove the muffin tin from the oven and allow the muffins to cool in the pan for 5 minutes, then remove from the pan and let them fully cool on a wire rack.
8. Serve and enjoy the gluten-free lemon poppy seed muffins warm, or store in an airtight container at room temperature for up to 3 days.

MANGO MUFFINS

Preparation Time: 20 minutes
Cooking Time: 25 minutes

INGREDIENTS:
- 2 ripe mangos, peeled and diced
- 2 cups of gluten-free all-purpose flour
- 1 cup of granulated sugar
- 1 teaspoon of baking soda
- 1 teaspoon of xanthan gum (omit if your flour blend has it)
- 1/2 teaspoon of salt
- 2 large eggs
- 1/2 cup of vegetable oil
- 1 teaspoon of pure vanilla extract
- 1/4 cup of almond milk (or any other dairy-free milk)

INSTRUCTIONS:
1. Preheat your oven to 350°F (175°C) and line a muffin pan with paper liners.
2. In a large bowl, combine the gluten-free flour, sugar, baking soda, xanthan gum (if using), and salt.
3. In another bowl, whisk together the eggs, oil, and vanilla extract until well combined.
4. Gradually add the dry ingredients to the wet ingredients, alternating with the almond milk. Stir until the batter is smooth and well blended.
5. Fold in the diced mangoes.
6. Distribute the batter evenly into the muffin pan, filling each liner about two-thirds full.
7. Bake for 25-30 minutes, or until a toothpick inserted into the center of a muffin comes out clean.
8. Allow the muffins to cool in the pan for 5 minutes, then transfer them to a wire rack to cool completely.

ORANGE CRANBERRY MUFFINS

Preparation Time: 20 minutes
Cooking Time: 25 minutes

INGREDIENTS:
- 2 cups gluten-free all-purpose flour
- 1 teaspoon baking soda
- 1/4 teaspoon salt

- 3/4 cup granulated sugar
- 1 cup fresh cranberries, chopped
- 1 cup orange juice
- Zest of two oranges
- 1/2 cup vegetable oil
- 1 egg
- 1 teaspoon vanilla extract

INSTRUCTIONS:
1. Preheat your oven to 375 degrees Fahrenheit. While it is heating, line a muffin tin with paper liners and set it aside.
2. In a large bowl, combine your gluten-free all-purpose flour, baking soda, salt, and granulated sugar. Stir these ingredients until they are properly mixed.
3. Add the chopped cranberries to the bowl and toss them until they are coated in the flour mixture. This step helps to keep them from sinking to the bottom of your muffins while they bake.
4. In a separate bowl, combine your orange juice, the zest from your oranges, vegetable oil, egg, and vanilla extract. Whisk these ingredients together until they are fully incorporated.
5. Pour the wet mixture into the bowl with the dry ingredients. Stir everything together until the mixture is just combined. Try not to over mix it, as this can cause the muffins to be dense.
6. Spoon the mixture into your lined muffin tins. Fill each about two-thirds of the way full.
7. Bake the muffins in your preheated oven for approximately 25 minutes. They are ready when a toothpick inserted into their centers comes out clean.
8. Once they are done, let them cool in the muffin tin for about 10 minutes. After this time, you can remove them from the tin and let them cool completely.

PUMPKIN SPICE MUFFINS

Preparation Time: 15 minutes
Cooking Time: 20 minutes

INGREDIENTS:
- 1 1/2 cups gluten-free all-purpose flour
- 1 1/2 teaspoons baking powder
- 1/2 teaspoon baking soda
- 1 teaspoon xanthan gum (if your flour doesn't include it)
- 2 teaspoons pumpkin spice

- 1/2 teaspoon salt
- 3/4 cup canned pumpkin puree
- 1/2 cup granulated sugar
- 1/2 cup brown sugar
- 1/2 cup vegetable oil
- 12 large eggs
- 1 1/4 cup milk
- 2 teaspoons pure vanilla extract

INSTRUCTIONS:
1. Preheat your oven to 350°F (180°C). Line a standard muffin tin with paper liners.
2. In a medium bowl, whisk together the gluten-free flour, baking powder, baking soda, xanthan gum (if using), pumpkin spice, and salt. Set aside.
3. In a large bowl, combine the pumpkin puree, granulated sugar, brown sugar, and vegetable oil. Beat until combined and smooth.
4. Beat in the eggs, one at a time, mixing well after each addition. Stir in the vanilla extract.
5. Gradually add the dry ingredients to the large bowl of wet ingredients, alternating with the milk. Begin and end with the dry ingredients. Mix just until the dry ingredients are fully incorporated.
6. Fill each muffin cup about 3/4 full of batter.
7. Bake in the preheated oven for about 20-25 minutes, or until a toothpick inserted into the center of a muffin comes out clean or with a few moist crumbs.
8. Let the muffins cool in the pan for 5 minutes before transferring them to a wire rack to cool completely.

RASPBERRY ALMOND MUFFINS

Preparation Time: 15 minutes
Cooking Time: 25 minutes

INGREDIENTS:
- 2 cups almond flour
- 1/2 cup sugar
- 3/4 tsp baking soda
- 1/4 tsp salt
- 3 large eggs
- 1/4 cup melted unsalted butter
- 1/4 cup unsweetened almond milk
- 1 tsp pure vanilla extract

- 1 cup fresh raspberries
- 1/4 cup sliced almonds

INSTRUCTIONS:
1. Preheat the oven to 350 degrees F (180 degrees C) and line a muffin tin with paper liners.
2. In a large bowl, combine the almond flour, sugar, baking soda, and salt. Stir until well mixed.
3. In a separate bowl, whisk together the eggs, melted butter, almond milk, and vanilla extract until fully combined.
4. Gradually mix the wet ingredients into the dry ingredients, stirring until just combined. Be careful not to over-mix.
5. Gently fold in the fresh raspberries so they don't get crushed.
6. Spoon batter into the prepared muffin tin, filling each cup about 3/4 full.
7. Sprinkle the top of each muffin with a few sliced almonds.
8. Bake for 25 minutes or until the muffins are lightly golden and a toothpick inserted into the center comes out clean.
9. Allow the muffins to cool in the tin for 10 minutes before removing them to finish cooling on a wire rack.

STRAWBERRY BANANA MUFFINS

Preparation Time: 15 minutes
Cooking Time: 25 minutes

INGREDIENTS:
- 1 1/2 cups of gluten-free flour
- 1 teaspoon of baking powder
- 1/2 teaspoon of baking soda
- 1/4 teaspoon of salt
- 1/2 cup of unsalted butter, at room temperature
- 1 cup of granulated sugar
- 2 large eggs
- 1 teaspoon of pure vanilla extract
- 2 ripe bananas, mashed
- 1/2 cup of buttermilk
- 1 cup of fresh strawberries, diced

INSTRUCTIONS:

1. Preheat your oven to 300 degrees F (185 degrees C). Line a muffin tin with paper liners or lightly grease and set aside.
2. In a large bowl, combine the gluten-free flour, baking powder, baking soda, and salt.
3. In a separate large bowl, using a hand mixer or a stand mixer fitted with a paddle attachment, cream together the butter and sugar until light and fluffy.
4. Beat in the eggs, one at a time, followed by the vanilla extract, mashed bananas, and buttermilk. Blend until well combined.
5. Gradually add the dry ingredients to the wet ingredients, stirring just until combined. The batter should be thickened.
6. Fold in the diced strawberries, stirring lightly to evenly distribute throughout the batter.
7. Using a spoon or ice-cream scoop, fill each muffin well 3/4 full with the batter.
8. Bake in the preheated oven for 20-25 minutes, or when a toothpick inserted into the center of a muffin comes out clean.
9. Allow the muffins to cool in the tin for 5 minutes before transferring to a wire rack to cool completely.

DELICIOUS SNACKS AND DELIGHTS

BAGELS

Preparation Time: 2 hours 30 minutes
Cooking Time: 25 minutes

INGREDIENTS:
- 1 1/2 cups of warm water
- 1 tablespoon of sugar
- 1 packet (2 1/4 teaspoons) of active dry yeast
- 3 1/2 cups of gluten-free bread flour
- 2 teaspoons of xanthan gum (omit if it's already in your bread mix)
- 1 1/2 teaspoons of salt
- 1 tablespoon of apple cider vinegar
- 2 tablespoons of olive oil for brushing
- Optional: poppy seeds, sesame seeds, or coarse salt for topping

INSTRUCTIONS:
1. Mix the warm water and sugar in a small bowl until the sugar is dissolved. Sprinkle the yeast on top of the water and set it aside for five minutes to activate.
2. In a large mixing bowl, combine the gluten-free bread flour, xanthan gum (if using), and salt.
3. After the yeast has activated (it will appear foamy on the surface), pour it into the dry mix along with the vinegar.
4. Use a spoon to combine the ingredients well, and then use your hands to knead the dough in the bowl. The dough should be firm but not dry.
5. Cover the bowl with a damp cloth and set it aside in a warm area for about 2 hours. The dough should roughly double in size.
6. Preheat your oven to 425 degrees and line a baking sheet with parchment paper.
7. Transfer the risen dough to a flour-dusted surface. Divide the dough into 8 equal pieces and roll each piece into a ball.
8. Press your thumb into the center of each ball to create a hole. Gently stretch and shape the dough into a bagel shape.
9. Arrange the shaped dough on the prepared baking sheet. Brush the tops of the bagels with olive oil and sprinkle your selected toppings over the bagels.
10. Bake the bagels for 25 minutes or until golden brown. Remove them from the oven and let them cool on a rack for at least 15 minutes before slicing and serving.

CHEESE PUFFS

Preparation Time: 15 minutes

Cooking Time: 20 minutes

INGREDIENTS:
- 1/2 cup of gluten-free flour
- 1/2 cup of cornstarch
- 1 teaspoon of baking powder
- 1 teaspoon of xanthan gum (omit if your flour blend already has it)
- 1/2 teaspoon of salt
- 1/4 teaspoon of ground black pepper
- 4 large eggs
- 1 cup of whole milk
- 2 cups of shredded cheddar cheese
- Optional: chives or any herb of choice for extra flavor

INSTRUCTIONS:
1. Preheat your oven to 400°F (200°C) and grease a mini muffin tin.
2. In a medium-sized bowl, combine the gluten-free flour, cornstarch, baking powder, xanthan gum (if using), salt, and black pepper.
3. In a separate large bowl, beat the eggs and then whisk in the milk.
4. Gradually add the dry ingredient mixture to the egg and milk mixture, whisking continuously to avoid lumps.
5. Stir in the shredded cheese (and herbs if using) until evenly distributed.
6. Spoon or pipe the batter into the prepared mini muffin tin, filling each cup just under the top.
7. Bake in the preheated oven for 20 minutes, or until the cheese puffs are golden brown and puffed up.
8. Allow them to cool slightly in the tin before removing.
9. Enjoy these gluten-free cheese puffs warm. Store any leftovers in an airtight container. They also freeze well for future snacking.

CHEESY BREADSTICKS

Preparation Time: 20 minutes
Cooking Time: 25 minutes

INGREDIENTS:
- 1 1/2 cups of gluten-free flour blend
- 2 teaspoons of xanthan gum (*do not add if your flour blend already contains it)
- 2 teaspoons of baking powder
- 1 teaspoon of salt

- 1 cup of warm water
- 2 tablespoons of olive oil
- 2 tablespoons of sugar
- 1 packet (or 2 1/4 teaspoons) of active dry yeast
- 1 teaspoon of garlic powder
- 1 teaspoon of dried oregano
- 1 teaspoon of dried basil
- 2 cups of shredded mozzarella cheese
- 2 tablespoons of grated Parmesan cheese

INSTRUCTIONS:
1. Preheat your oven to 425 degrees Fahrenheit (218° C)and lightly grease a baking sheet.
2. In a large bowl, combine gluten-free flour, xanthan gum, baking powder, and salt. Mix well.
3. In a separate bowl, mix warm water, olive oil, and sugar. Stir until the sugar is dissolved.
4. Sprinkle the yeast over the water mixture, do not stir. Let it sit for 5 minutes until yeast becomes frothy.
5. Pour the yeast mixture into the dry ingredients and stir until smooth.
6. Spread the dough on the prepared baking sheet and shape it into a rectangle of about 1/2-inch thickness.
7. Let the dough sit for about 10 minutes to rise.
8. Sprinkle the dough with garlic powder, oregano, basil, then evenly cover it with shredded mozzarella and sprinkle with Parmesan cheese.
9. Bake in the preheated oven for 18-20 minutes, or until the cheese is melted and bubbly and the edges of the breadsticks are lightly golden.
10. Remove from oven and let cool for a couple of minutes before cutting into breadsticks.

CHOCOLATE BANANA BREAD

Preparation Time: 20 minutes
Cooking Time: 60 minutes

INGREDIENTS:
- 3 ripe bananas
- 2 large eggs
- 1/4 cup of unsalted butter, melted
- 1/4 cup of natural unsweetened cocoa powder

- 1 1/4 cup of gluten-free flour
- 3/4 cup of light brown sugar
- 1 teaspoon of vanilla extract
- 1 teaspoon of baking soda
- 1/2 teaspoon of salt
- 1 cup of semi-sweet chocolate chips

INSTRUCTIONS:
1. Start by preheating your oven to 350°F (175°C). Grease and line a 9x5 inch loaf pan with parchment paper.
2. In a large bowl, mash the bananas until smooth. You can use a fork to make this easier.
3. Add the melted butter, eggs, and vanilla extract to the mashed bananas and mix until well combined.
4. In another bowl, combine the gluten-free flour, cocoa powder, light brown sugar, baking soda, and salt. Stir well to mix the dry ingredients.
5. Gradually mix the dry ingredients into the wet ingredients until the batter is smooth. Be careful not to overmix; a few lumps are ok.
6. Fold in the chocolate chips until they are evenly dispersed through the batter.
7. Pour the batter into the prepared loaf pan, spreading it evenly with the back of your spoon.
8. Bake in the preheated oven for approximately 60 minutes, until a skewer inserted into the center of the loaf comes out mostly clean. If the top begins to darken too much before the center is done, cover with aluminum foil.
9. Once done, allow the bread to cool in the pan for 10 minutes before transferring to a wire rack to cool completely.

CHOCOLATE CHIP BREAD

Preparation Time: 15 minutes
Cooking Time: 60 minutes

INGREDIENTS:
- 2 cups gluten-free all-purpose flour
- 1 cup granulated sugar
- 1 teaspoon baking powder
- 1/2 teaspoon baking soda
- 1/4 teaspoon salt
- 1/2 cup unsalted butter, melted and cooled
- 2 large eggs

- 1 teaspoon pure vanilla extract
- 1 cup buttermilk (or homemade substitute: add 1 Tbsp lemon juice to 1 cup milk and leave for 10 minutes)
- 1 cup semi-sweet chocolate chips

INSTRUCTIONS:
1. Preheat your oven to 350°F (175°C). Grease a 9x5 inch loaf pan and set aside.
2. In a large bowl, whisk together the gluten-free flour, sugar, baking powder, baking soda, and salt.
3. In a separate bowl, combine the melted butter, eggs, and vanilla extract. Whisk until fully combined.
4. Gradually add the wet ingredients to the dry ingredients, mixing just until combined.
5. Stir in the buttermilk until the batter is smooth.
6. Fold in the chocolate chips.
7. Pour the batter into the prepared loaf pan and spread it out evenly with a spatula.
8. Bake for about 60 minutes, or until a toothpick inserted into the center of the bread comes out clean. Let the bread cool in the pan for 10 minutes, then transfer it to a wire rack to cool completely.
9. Slice and serve your gluten-free chocolate chip bread at room temperature. Enjoy as a delicious dessert or a sweet breakfast treat!

CHOCOLATE SWIRL BREAD

Preparation Time: 20 minutes
Cooking Time: 50 minutes

INGREDIENTS:
- 2 cups of gluten-free flour
- 3/4 cup of granulated sugar
- 1 tablespoon of baking powder
- 1/2 teaspoon of salt
- 1 cup of milk
- 1/4 cup of unsalted butter, melted
- 2 large eggs
- 1 teaspoon of vanilla extract
- 1/3 cup of unsweetened cocoa powder
- 3 tablespoons of boiling water
- 1/2 cup of semi-sweet chocolate chips

INSTRUCTIONS:

1. Preheat the oven to 350°F (175°C). Lightly grease a 9x5 inch loaf pan with butter or cooking spray, then set it aside.
2. In a large bowl, combine the gluten-free flour, sugar, baking powder, and salt. Stir until all ingredients are well distributed.
3. In a separate bowl, whisk together the milk, melted butter, eggs, and vanilla extract. Gradually add this mixture to the dry ingredients, stirring until the batter is smooth.
4. Split the batter into two equal halves. In one half, add the cocoa powder and boiling water. Stir it well to create a smooth chocolate batter.
5. Drop large spoonsful of the plain and chocolate batters alternately into the prepared loaf pan. Gently swirl the two batters together using a knife or a spoon. Sprinkle the top with chocolate chips.
6. Bake the bread in the preheated oven for 50-60 minutes, or until a toothpick inserted into the center comes out clean. Let the bread cool in the pan for 10 minutes, then turn it out onto a wire rack to cool completely.
7. Slice and serve your gluten-free chocolate swirl bread. Enjoy it as a delightful dessert or a sweet start to your day!

CINNAMON SUGAR DONUT HOLES

Preparation Time: 10 minutes
Cooking Time: 10 minutes

INGREDIENTS:
- 1 cup gluten-free all-purpose flour
- 1/4 cup granulated sugar
- 1/2 teaspoon ground cinnamon
- 1/2 teaspoon nutmeg
- 1/2 teaspoon baking powder
- 1/4 teaspoon baking soda
- 1/2 teaspoon salt
- 1/2 cup buttermilk
- 1 egg
- 3 tablespoons unsalted butter, melted
- 1 teaspoon pure vanilla extract

FOR THE CINNAMON SUGAR:
- 1/2 cup granulated sugar
- 1 tablespoon ground cinnamon
- 3 tablespoons unsalted butter, melted

INSTRUCTIONS:
1. Preheat your oven to 375°F (190°C) and lightly grease a 24-cup mini muffin tin.
2. In a large bowl, whisk together the gluten-free flour, sugar, cinnamon, nutmeg, baking powder, baking soda, and salt.
3. In a separate bowl, combine the buttermilk, egg, melted butter, and vanilla extract.
4. Slowly add the wet ingredients to the dry ones and stir until combined. The batter will appear slightly lumpy, that's okay.
5. Spoon the batter into the prepared muffin tin, filling each cup about 2/3 full.
6. Bake in the preheated oven for 10-12 minutes, or until a toothpick inserted into the center of the donuts comes out clean.
7. While the donuts are baking, prepare the cinnamon sugar topping. In a small bowl, mix the sugar and cinnamon.
8. Once the donuts are done, let them cool in the tin for 5 minutes before transferring to a wire rack.
9. Dip the warm donut holes in the melted butter, then roll in the cinnamon sugar mixture until evenly coated.

CORNBREAD MUFFINS

Preparation Time: 15 minutes
Cooking Time: 20 minutes

INGREDIENTS:
- 1 cup gluten-free cornmeal
- 1 cup gluten-free all-purpose flour
- 4 teaspoons of gluten-free baking powder
- 1/4 cup of white sugar
- 1/2 teaspoon of salt
- 1 cup of milk (you can use dairy-free if needed)
- 1 large egg
- 1/4 cup of unsalted butter, melted

INSTRUCTIONS:
1. Preheat the oven to 425°F (220°C) and line a regular muffin tin with 12 liners.
2. In a large bowl, mix the gluten-free cornmeal, gluten-free all-purpose flour, baking powder, sugar, and salt.
3. In a separate bowl, whisk together the milk and egg. Stir in the melted butter.
4. Gradually add the wet ingredients into the dry ingredients, stirring just until combined.
5. Pour the batter evenly into the muffin cups.

6. Bake in the preheated oven for 15-20 minutes or until the muffins are golden brown and a toothpick inserted into the center comes out clean.
7. Allow the muffins to cool for 5 minutes before removing them from the tin. Enjoy these gluten-free cornbread muffins warm or at room temperature.

GARLIC KNOTS

Preparation Time: 25 minutes
Cooking Time: 25 minutes

INGREDIENTS:
For the dough:
- 2 1/4 cups gluten-free flour blend
- 2 teaspoons xanthan gum (only if your mix doesn't already contain it)
- 1 packet (about 2 1/4 teaspoons) rapid rise yeast
- 1 tablespoon granulated sugar
- 1 teaspoon salt
- 1 cup warm water (105-110°F)
- 2 tablespoons extra virgin olive oil
- 1 teaspoon cider vinegar

For the garlic butter coating:
- 4 cloves garlic, finely minced
- 2 tablespoons extra virgin olive oil
- 2 tablespoons unsalted butter
- 1/4 teaspoon salt
- 1/4 teaspoon dried parsley flakes

INSTRUCTIONS:
1. Begin by mixing the gluten-free flour blend, xanthan gum (if needed), instant yeast, sugar, and salt together in a large bowl.
2. In another bowl, combine the warm water, olive oil, and cider vinegar and then add this mixture to the dry mix.
3. Mix until the dough just comes together. It should be sticky but not liquid. If necessary, add a bit more water or flour.
4. Cover the bowl with plastic wrap and let it rest in a warm place for about 15 minutes.
5. Preheat the oven to 425°F while the dough is resting, and line a baking sheet with parchment paper.
6. Turn the dough onto a floured surface and divide it into 12 equal pieces.
7. Roll each piece of dough, then tie into a simple knot.

8. Arrange the knots on the baking sheet and bake them for 10 to 15 minutes, or until they're lightly golden brown.
9. While they are baking, combine the minced garlic, olive oil, butter, and salt in a saucepan over medium heat. Cook the mixture until the butter is melted and the garlic is fragrant.
10. Pour the garlic butter over the baked knots as soon as they come out of the oven, make sure you get as much of the garlic on the knots as possible.
11. Sprinkle the knots with the dried parsley for extra flavor and color.
12. Serve these beautiful gluten-free garlic knots warm with your favorite dipping sauce or alongside a hearty Italian dish. Enjoy!

MINI PIZZA CRUSTS

Preparation Time: 15 minutes
Cooking Time: 15 minutes

INGREDIENTS:
- 2 cups of gluten-free all-purpose flour
- 1 tablespoon of sugar
- 1 teaspoon of salt
- 1 tablespoon of quick-rise yeast
- 1 teaspoon of xanthan gum (skip if your gluten-free flour includes it)
- 1 cup of warm water (110-115 degrees Fahrenheit)
- 1 tablespoon of olive oil
- 1/2 teaspoon of apple cider vinegar
- Cooking spray for greasing

INSTRUCTIONS:
1. In a large bowl, combine the gluten-free flour, sugar, salt, yeast, and xanthan gum. Stir these ingredients until they are well mixed.
2. In a separate bowl, combine the warm water, olive oil, and apple cider vinegar.
3. Gradually add the liquid mixture to the dry ingredients, stirring continuously. The final dough should be slightly sticky, but not too wet.
4. Lightly dust a clean working surface with some gluten-free flour. Turn out the dough onto this surface and knead for a few minutes. If the dough is too sticky, add a bit more flour.
5. Preheat your oven to 425 degrees Fahrenheit and grease a baking sheet with cooking spray.
6. Divide your dough into four equal parts. Roll each part into a ball, then flatten each into a thin disc about 1/4 inch thick. These are your mini pizza crusts.

7. Place the crusts onto the prepared baking sheet. Bake in the preheated oven for around 10-12 minutes, or until the crusts are lightly golden and firm to the touch.
8. The crusts are now ready to be topped with your favorite pizza sauces, cheeses, and toppings, then returned to the oven to melt the cheese and bake the toppings.
9. Enjoy your homemade gluten-free mini pizza crusts!

MONKEY BREAD

Preparation Time: 35 minutes
Cooking Time: 30 minutes

INGREDIENTS:
- 3 cups gluten-free flour
- 2 tsp xanthan gum (if your flour blend doesn't include it)
- 3 tsp baking powder
- 1/2 tsp salt
- 2 tbsp granulated sugar
- 1/2 cup unsalted butter (melted and cooled)
- 3/4 cup milk (lukewarm)
- 1 large egg (room temperature)

For the Coating:
- 1/2 cup unsalted butter (melted)
- 1 cup granulated sugar
- 2 tsp cinnamon

INSTRUCTIONS:
1. Preheat your oven to 350°F (175°C). Grease a bundt pan using gluten-free cooking spray or a brush of melted butter.
2. In a large bowl, whisk together gluten-free flour, xanthan gum (if using), baking powder, salt, and sugar.
3. In a separate smaller bowl, combine melted and cooled butter, lukewarm milk, and the egg.
4. Gradually add the liquid mixture into the flour mixture and stir until you have a smooth, sticky dough.
5. Roll the dough into 1-inch balls.
6. In another bowl, combine the melted butter, granulated sugar, and cinnamon to make the coating.
7. Dip each dough ball into the coating mixture, making sure it's fully covered before placing it in the prepared bundt pan.

8. Once all dough balls are in the pan, pour over any remaining coating mixture.
9. Bake for 30 minutes, or until the bread is golden and bubbly.
10. Allow the bread to cool in the pan for 10 minutes before transferring it to a cooling rack.
11. Your gluten-free monkey bread is ready to serve! It's best enjoyed warm.

PANCAKE BITES

Preparation Time: 15 minutes
Cooking Time: 10 minutes

INGREDIENTS:
- 1 cup gluten-free all-purpose flour
- 2 tablespoons granulated sugar
- 1 teaspoon gluten-free baking powder
- 1/2 teaspoon baking soda
- 1/4 teaspoon salt
- 3/4 cup buttermilk
- 1 large egg
- 3 tablespoons unsalted butter, melted and cooled
- 1 teaspoon vanilla extract
- Cooking spray or additional melted butter for greasing

INSTRUCTIONS:
1. In a large mixing bowl, whisk together the flour, sugar, baking powder, baking soda, and salt.
2. In a separate, smaller bowl, whisk together the buttermilk, egg, melted butter, and vanilla extract.
3. Pour the wet ingredients into the dry ingredients and stir them together until they are just combined.
4. Preheat your pancake bite pan over medium heat and lightly coat with cooking spray or a small dab of butter.
5. Using a spoon or a small scoop, fill each well of the pan about three-quarters full of batter.
6. Cook the pancake bites for 2-3 minutes, or until you see the edges are beginning to darken and curl.
7. Flip each pancake bite using a fork or a skewer and continue cooking for another 2-3 minutes or until golden brown and cooked through.
8. Remove the pancake bites from the pan and keep them warm while you prepare the rest of the batter.

9. Serve the gluten-free pancake bites warm with syrup, fresh fruits or your favorite jam for a delightful gluten-free breakfast or snack.

PIZZA ROLLS

Preparation Time: 25 minutes
Cooking Time: 20 minutes

INGREDIENTS:
For the dough:
- 2 cups of gluten-free flour
- 1 tsp of xanthan gum (not necessary if your gluten-free flour blend already includes it)
- 2 tsp of baking powder
- A pinch of salt
- 3/4 cup of water
- 1 tbsp of olive oil

For the filling:
- 1 cup of tomato sauce
- 2 cups of shredded mozzarella cheese
- 1 cup of sliced pepperoni (ensure it's gluten-free)
- 1/2 tsp of dried oregano
- 1/2 tsp of garlic powder

INSTRUCTIONS:
- Preheat your oven to 375°F (190°C) and line a baking sheet with parchment paper.
- In a large bowl, combine the gluten-free flour, xanthan gum (if using), baking powder, and salt.
- Gradually add water and olive oil to the mixture, stirring until a dough forms. If the dough is too sticky, add a bit more flour. If it's too dry, add a bit more water.
- On a floured surface, roll out the dough into a rectangle, about 1/4 inch thick.
- Spread the tomato sauce evenly over the dough, leaving about a 1/2 inch border all around.
- Sprinkle the shredded cheese, pepperoni slices, oregano, and garlic powder evenly over the tomato sauce.
- Starting from one of the shorter sides of the rectangle, gently roll up the dough into a log.
- Slice the log into 12-15 pieces and place the rolls on the prepared baking sheet.

- Bake for 20 minutes, or until the crust is golden and the cheese is bubbly and slightly browned.
- Allow the pizza rolls to cool slightly before serving. Enjoy these gluten-free pizza rolls while warm!

POPOVERS

Preparation Time: 15 minutes
Cooking Time: 30 minutes

INGREDIENTS:
- 1 cup of gluten-free flour blend
- 1/2 teaspoon of xanthan gum (omit if your flour blend already contains it)
- 1/2 teaspoon of salt
- 4 large eggs
- 1 cup of whole milk
- 2 tablespoons of unsalted butter, melted
- Cooking spray for the muffin tin

INSTRUCTIONS:
1. Preheat your oven to 425°F (220°C).
2. Apply the cooking spray inside a 12 cup muffin tin, coating well and evenly to ensure the popovers do not stick.
3. In a large bowl, combine the gluten-free flour blend, xanthan gum (if using), and salt.
4. In another bowl, beat the eggs until they're light and foamy.
5. Gradually pour the milk into the beaten eggs, whisking consistently until well-mixed.
6. Slowly add the dry ingredients to the egg and milk mixture, whisking to combine. Make sure there are no lumps.
7. Stir in the melted butter.
8. Pour the batter evenly into the prepared muffin cups. Fill each only halfway to make sure the popovers have enough space to rise.
9. Place the muffin tin in the preheated oven and bake for 30 minutes, or until the popovers are golden and puffy.
10. Remove the popovers from the oven and immediately take them out of the pan to stop them from becoming soggy.
11. Popovers are best served fresh out of the oven. Enjoy them with a spread of butter or a dollop of your favorite jam.

PUMPKIN BREAD

Preparation Time: 20 minutes
Cooking Time: 65 minutes

INGREDIENTS:
- 1 3/4 cups gluten-free all-purpose flour
- 1 1/2 teaspoons gluten-free baking powder
- 1 teaspoon baking soda
- 1/2 teaspoon salt
- 1 1/2 teaspoons ground cinnamon
- 1/2 teaspoon ground nutmeg
- 1/4 teaspoon ground cloves
- 1/2 cup brown sugar, packed
- 2 large eggs
- 1 cup canned pumpkin puree
- 1/2 cup vegetable oil
- 1/4 cup milk (dairy or non-dairy, both work)
- 1 teaspoon pure vanilla extract

INSTRUCTIONS:
1. Preheat your oven to 350°F (175°C) and line a 9x5-inch loaf pan with parchment paper.
2. In a large bowl, whisk together the gluten-free all-purpose flour, baking powder, baking soda, salt, cinnamon, nutmeg, and cloves until well blended.
3. In a separate bowl, combine the brown sugar, eggs, pumpkin puree, oil, milk, and vanilla. Stir until fully mixed.
4. Gradually add the dry ingredients into the wet ingredients, stirring until just combined. Make sure not to overmix as this can result in a tough bread.
5. Pour the batter into the prepared loaf pan and smooth the top with a spatula.
6. Bake in the preheated oven for about 65 minutes, or until a toothpick inserted into the center of the bread comes out clean.
7. Allow the bread to cool in the pan for about 15 minutes before removing. Then, transfer it to a wire rack to finish cooling.
8. Once cooled completely, slice and serve. Enjoy the delicious and moist gluten-free pumpkin bread, perfect for any time of the day!

PRETZEL BITES

Preparation Time: 20 minutes

Cooking Time: 15 minutes

INGREDIENTS:
- 2 cups of gluten-free all-purpose flour
- 1 packet (or 2 1/4 teaspoons) of active dry yeast
- 1 teaspoon of salt
- 1 tablespoon of sugar
- 1 cup of warm water (approximately 110°F)
- 1 tablespoon of olive oil
- 1/2 cup of baking soda
- Coarse sea salt for topping
- 4 cups of water for boiling

INSTRUCTIONS:
1. In a large bowl combine the gluten-free flour, yeast, salt, and sugar. Slowly add the warm water and olive oil while stirring the mixture using a spoon or a spatula.
2. Once the dough starts to form, use your hands to knead it until it's smooth and slightly sticky. Let the dough rest for 15 minutes.
3. Preheat your oven to 450°F and line a baking sheet with parchment paper.
4. Bring the 4 cups of water to a boil in a large saucepan. Carefully add the baking soda to the boiling water (it will bubble up rapidly).
5. While waiting for the water to boil, divide the dough into small bite-sized pieces.
6. Once the water is boiling, drop a handful of dough pieces into the water. Let them cook for about 30 seconds then use a slotted spoon to transfer them onto the prepared baking sheet.
7. Repeat with the remaining dough pieces, ensuring they're not touching on the baking sheet.
8. Sprinkle each pretzel bite with coarse sea salt, then bake for approximately 15 minutes or until they become golden brown.
9. Remove them from the oven and allow them to cool slightly before serving.

SOFT PRETZELS

Preparation Time: 45 minutes
Cooking Time: 15 minutes

INGREDIENTS:
- 1 packet (2 1/4 teaspoons) dry active yeast
- 1 teaspoon honey
- 1 cup warm water (110°F)

- 2 cups gluten-free flour blend
- 1 teaspoon xanthan gum (omit if your flour blend contains it)
- 1 teaspoon baking powder
- 1 teaspoon salt
- 1 tablespoon apple cider vinegar
- 2 tablespoons extra virgin olive oil
- Kosher salt for sprinkling on top
- 1/4 cup baking soda (for the boiling water bath)

INSTRUCTIONS
1. In a small bowl, combine the yeast, warm water, and honey. Let it stand for about 5 minutes to activate the yeast. It should become frothy.
2. In a large mixing bowl, combine the gluten-free flour blend, xanthan gum if using, baking powder, and salt. Stir to combine.
3. Create a well in the middle of the dry ingredients and add the apple cider vinegar, olive oil, and yeast mixture. Stir to form a sticky dough.
4. Turn the dough onto a surface lightly dusted with gluten-free flour. Knead for 1-2 minutes until the dough is smooth and no longer sticky.
5. Preheat your oven to 425°F and line a baking sheet with parchment paper.
6. Divide the dough into 8 equal pieces. Roll each piece into a long rope, about 14 inches long. Form it into a pretzel shape and place on the prepared baking sheet.
7. In a large pot, bring 8 cups of water to a boil. Slowly add the baking soda to the boiling water.
8. Carefully lower each pretzel into the boiling water bath using a slotted spatula. Boil for about 30 seconds on each side. Remove them from the water and place back onto the baking sheet.
9. Sprinkle each pretzel with kosher salt and bake for 15 minutes, or until golden brown.
10. Let them cool on the baking sheet for a few minutes before enjoying warm with your favorite dipping sauce.
11. Remember, these pretzels are best enjoyed on the day they are made. Enjoy!

STRAWBERRY SHORTCAKE BISCUITS

Preparation Time: 30 minutes
Cooking Time: 20 minutes

INGREDIENTS:
- 2 cups of gluten-free all-purpose flour
- 1/4 cup of granulated sugar

- 1 tablespoon of baking powder
- 1/2 teaspoon of salt
- 1/2 cup of cold unsalted butter, cut into small pieces
- 2/3 cup of cold milk substitute (almond milk, coconut milk, etc.)
- 1 teaspoon of pure vanilla extract
- 1 egg
- 1 pound of fresh strawberries, hulled and halved
- 1 cup of whipped cream (optional)

INSTRUCTIONS:

1. Preheat your oven to 425 degrees Fahrenheit and line a baking sheet with parchment paper.
2. In a large bowl, whisk together the gluten-free flour, sugar, baking powder, and salt.
3. Use a pastry blender or two forks to cut in the cold butter until the mixture resembles coarse crumbs.
4. Stir in the cold milk substitute and vanilla extract until just combined.
5. Turn out the dough on a lightly floured (with gluten-free flour) surface and knead it a few times to bring it together.
6. Roll or pat the dough out to about 1-inch thickness. Using a biscuit cutter or glass, cut biscuits out of the dough and place them on the prepared baking sheet.
7. Beat the egg in a small bowl and brush the tops of the biscuits with the beaten egg.
8. Bake in the preheated oven for 15 to 20 minutes, or until the biscuits are golden and baked through.
9. While the biscuits are baking, place the strawberries in a bowl and sprinkle with some sugar if desired, let them sit to juice out.
10. Once the biscuits have cooled slightly, slice them in half horizontally. Spoon some strawberries onto each bottom half, then add a dollop of whipped cream if desired.
11. Place the top half of the biscuit on the strawberries and cream and serve immediately.

THANK YOU FROM THE BOTTOM OF MY HEART

Thank you for joining me on this delightful journey through the world of gluten-free bread baking. I hope you have found inspiration and joy in each recipe, discovering new ways to bring delicious, nutritious gluten-free delights to your family's table. Remember, the kitchen is your playground—don't hesitate to experiment and put your unique spin on these recipes.

Continue baking, exploring, and nurturing your passion for creating wholesome baked goods. Happy baking and may your gluten-free adventures be continuously rewarding!

With gratitude and best wishes,
Emma Brooks

By the way, do not forget to grab your 3 free bonuses. Scan the QR code below!
1. Gluten-Free Flour Formula: 8 Flour Blends for Perfect Bakes
2. Texture Triumph Toolkit: Real Bread Texture Every Time
3. Busy Baker's Bible: 10 Time-Saving Hacks for Effortless Gluten-Free Baking

Made in the USA
Monee, IL
22 December 2024